THE PRESIDENCY

☆☆☆☆☆

DALE VINYARD

THE PRESIDENCY

☆☆☆☆☆

CHARLES SCRIBNER'S SONS
New York

ACKNOWLEDGMENTS

I wish to take this opportunity to express my appreciation to those who played some role in the development and preparation of this volume:

To a long list of teachers who stimulated and encouraged me on the way, most notably, Millie A. Wright, Leland H. Carlson and Ralph K. Huitt.

To numerous students, first at Wisconsin State University, Platteville and later at Wayne State University who may have felt many times that they were being subjected to "cruel and unusual punishments."

To Marina Prinos, who had the worst task of all—trying to determine what those scratchings on a yellow pad might mean.

And to Jo Ellen who, as always, was there—the greatest gift of all.

*To the memory of my Mother and Father
which will never die.*

PREFACE

In the last few years the presidency as an institution and the occupants of that office have come under fairly heavy attack and criticism. For example, a recent book on the presidency was ominously entitled *The Twilight of the Presidency*.[1] During the 1968 presidential campaign, one candidate, Senator Eugene McCarthy articulated the concern of many about a strong, activist president. While such criticism is not entirely new, what is new is the amount and the duration of such criticism, perhaps, the volume as well.

One factor which is new is that criticism of the presidency is not confined to conservatives, but is voiced by some liberals as well.[2] At least since the 1930s conservatives have been wary of strong, activist presidents and their alleged invasion of the prerogatives of the other branches, particularly Congress. But, on the whole, liberals have been supporters of strong, activist presidents and critical of an incumbent (e.g., Eisenhower) when he adopted a fairly limited view of his powers. But in the late 1960s some liberals found themselves deeply troubled by the action of a strong president, specifically over the issue of Vietnam, and questioned some of their own previous views.

Nor is the presidency alone as an object of criticism and questioning; rather in the 1960s many of our other basic in-

1. See George E. Reedy, *The Twilight of the Presidency* (New York: World Publishing Co., 1970).
2. For an example of such liberal doubts, see Arthur Schlesinger, jr., "The Limits and Excesses of Presidential Power," *Saturday Review*, May 3, 1969, 17.

stitutions have come under attack. While some criticism is wholly negative, ill-informed and destructive, other consists of thoughtful and searching examinations of our institutions and their viability in the modern world.

The purpose of this volume is to provide the reader with an introduction to the American presidency, so that he may understand the functions of the office, its relation to other participants in the policy-making process and its powers and limitations. It is also hoped that it will stimulate him to read further and more widely. (The Notes for each chapter as well as the Bibliography at the end of the book provide numerous suggestions.) On the basis of such knowledge, he will be better able to understand some of the problems of the modern president and to evaluate some of the criticisms and reforms.

CONTENTS

THE PRESIDENCY

☆☆☆☆☆

"God, what a job!" [1]

—WARREN G. HARDING

The presidency "requires the constitution of an athlete, the patience of a mother, the endurance of an early Christian." [2]

—WOODROW WILSON

This job "is like riding a tiger. A man has to keep riding or be swallowed." [3]

—HARRY S. TRUMAN

"What, currently, is the American Presidency? A cat on a hot tin roof." [4]

—RICHARD E. NEUSTADT

1

THE FUNCTIONS
OF THE PRESIDENCY

I do solemnly swear (or affirm) that I will faithfully execute the office of President of the United States, and will to the best of my ability preserve, protect and defend the Constitution of the United States.

With these hallowed words from Article II, Section 1, of the Constitution every four years a man takes up or renews for himself the burdens and duties of the presidency. This position has been characterized in various ways: as the most powerful in history, virtually a modern Caesar, as the most frustrating, an impossible task, a man-killing job, as the central command post of our political system. But no matter how it is described, no one can deny its importance, centrality and visibility in our political system.

Like most political institutions, the presidency performs a number of functions and shares each function to an extent with other institutions.[5] This is inevitable since the political process is too complex to fit into tidy, exclusive compartments. Instead, the entire process is untidy, with greater involvement and interaction among different institutions than the formal powers and procedures suggest.

☆
THE PRESIDENT AS A SYMBOL

One function which the president performs is that of a national symbol. An aspect of this is seen in the president's ceremonial duties—somewhat akin to those of the monarch in Great Britain, which may range from the most majestic and solemn, those almost of a politico-religious character, to the most tawdry and demeaning imaginable. Thus, a president may confer medals on national heroes, such as the spacemen, welcome foreign visitors or throw out the first ball at the opening game of the baseball season, etc. In the past, one ceremony endured by many presidents was their induction into an Indian tribe with the conferring of its war bonnet. Such moments of presidential discomfiture were then recorded for posterity by camera. Even today, a president will participate in the festivities of various ethnic and religious groups which may include the consumption of such diverse foods as to constitute a gastronomical nightmare.

The performance of these ceremonial chores, often called "the chief of state" role, may seem rather trivial and certainly very demanding of an important, but limited, presidential resource—time, but the president's function as a symbol is more than just the performance of such duties.[6] In a real sense the president, especially a popular and attractive incumbent, is, for many persons, a personification of the political system; he is someone with whom people can identify.[7] Through his words and deeds, he can share their hopes and difficulties, their victories and defeats. He can offer reassurance in times of trouble and doubt and proclaim their jubilation at the moments of victory or achievement. In him as a spokesman, many may find an image of what they think their nation was, is or ought to be. Woodrow Wilson once said: "Whatever strength I have and whatever authority I possess are mine only so long as I express the spirit and purpose of the American people." [8]

There are several other aspects to the symbolic character

of the presidency. Through his ceremonial activities and public curiosity about his, and his family's, private as well as
public life, many citizens find an outlet for emotional ex-
pression. It is easy to become engrossed in the drama (often
verging on the soap opera variety) and pageantry of the presidency. People *want* to know what the first family is doing,
who they are seeing, what they are eating, wearing, etc. The
courtship and marriage of a president's daughter, however
uncomfortable it may be for the principals, becomes a front-
page story. The tastes of a first lady in hats, shoes or coiffures
may be adopted by others as well. Thus the president and his
family are exposed to the demanding, often cruel, glare of the
public spotlight much as movie stars and sports celebrities.

For busy citizens, the president may provide a means of
reducing the complexity of the political process to a simpler
form, a cognitive handle to provide them with some sense of
what the government is doing. Thus, it may be Kennedy's
trade bill, Johnson's war on poverty, Nixon's welfare reforms
or unhappily, an Eisenhower recession or Johnson's war. The
policy-making process with its diversity of participants and
complexity of causal factors may be too impersonal, obscure
and complex for many to comprehend. On the other hand,
the president is very visible and personal—a convenient and
simple object of praise or blame.

The president may also serve as a symbol of national unity.
Thus in times of grave international peril or crisis, such as a
war, there is a compelling call to support the president and
present a united national front to the world. At the time of
the Cuban missile crisis, which put the United States in grave
danger of a nuclear confrontation with the Soviet Union, the
normal political life of the nation was suspended as it watched
with awe the almost personal confrontation of President
Kennedy and Soviet Premier Khrushchev. On the other hand,
during the Vietnam crisis, such attempted utilization of the
presidency, although frequent and strident, has been much less
successful.

Another symbolic aspect of the presidency is the attempt

to have him be a spokesman and trustee for the broader good of the community against more narrowly based partisan, sectional or economic interests. At the call of the president such groups are expected to eschew such "selfish interests" and unite in serving the common good. For example, in 1962, President John Kennedy as the symbol and representative of the "common good" forced the steel industry to reconsider and finally alter its decision to raise prices. But such attempts are not always as successful. And indeed presidents themselves at times have attempted to camouflage a narrow interest, such as a partisan cause, with the stamp of the common good.

Finally the president serves as a symbol of the stability and continuity of the political order. Although each occupant of the office brings a personal dimension to it and may, in some ways, permanently alter it, the presidential office has deep roots in tradition and custom. Such a historical basis links a particular incumbent to his predecessors and increases the awe and veneration for the office and its current occupant. In addition, the fact that there are regularized procedures for transferring its powers from one occupant to the next has provided the presidency with the proof of stability. Even after a closely contested election, such as the 1960 clash between John Kennedy and Richard Nixon, the results were peacefully accepted. Although the subsequent assassination of President Kennedy in 1963 was tragic and cruel, the transition to Vice-President Lyndon Johnson was peaceful and without the paralyzing disruptions that commonly occur in some other countries.

THE PRESIDENT IN
THE POLICY-MAKING PROCESS

Unlike the modern British monarch who also serves as a symbol, the president performs other functions in our political system, including his constitutional duties in the policy-making process. Basically, there are three closely related functions: 1) policy application; 2) policy initiation; and 3) policy advocacy.

The first of these, policy application, is of long standing and widely accepted. It is the traditional role prescribed to the executive by political theorists and constitution-makers. Thus, according to the doctrine of separation of powers, the familiar trilogy of legislative, executive and judicial powers, the function of the executive is to apply the laws, not make them. The Constitution charges the president in Article II "to take care that the laws be faithfully executed." Some presidents have, indeed, seen this as their primary obligation. For example, Herbert Hoover declared: "the first duty of the President under his oath of office is to secure the enforcement of the laws." [9] And probably no man in our history brought to the presidency greater administrative talents or experience than did Hoover. His relative lack of success as president suggests that other tasks may be as, if not more, important than the administrative.

In addition, the vast expansion of governmental services and regulations and their concomitant feature—the development of a vast federal bureaucracy—has made effective performance of this task difficult. No man can singlehandedly supervise this sprawling establishment on a day-to-day basis. Rather he must delegate such tasks to others, setting general guidelines and stepping in on occasion, if the need arises, to rectify a troublesome situation. Undoubtedly, as a result, some agencies escape effective superintendence. Some agencies by statute have been made largely independent of presidential control. Other agencies, through the support of powerful clientele groups, have won *de facto* independence from the president by making the political costs of such intervention too high.

Even the nature of the administrative task has changed. Modern legislatures frequently pass laws in largely skeletal form, conferring vast discretionary authority on administrators. For example, in the Trade Expansion Act of 1962, the president was given the authority, among other things, to reduce or raise import duties, or in some cases to eliminate them entirely. He was also authorized to provide relief to domestic concerns that he felt were suffering as a result of the application of the law. This is not atypical. Many laws provide few, if any, guidelines to the president in filling in the details other than vague directives to "serve the public interest" or "be fair, just, and reasonable." Such skeletal laws are justified on a number of grounds: the need for greater expertise than is possessed in the legislature, the need for continuous attention and the burden such detail would place on an already over-burdened legislature. At times, however, such laws provide a means of transferring a conflict to another political arena either because the legislature did not know what to do or could not placate the diverse interests involved in the controversy. But, regardless of the cause, such laws alter the very nature of the traditional administrative process.

Such developments inevitably lead us into the president's role as a policy initiator, for in such instances, he, or his subordinate, is not just applying the policy of others—he is, in fact, formulating policy. The president's policy initiation is also seen in his role as "chief legislator." To a considerable extent, the agenda of each Congress is the president's legislative program. True, many of these ideas are not original with him; they were culled in many instances from administrative agencies, interest groups and, in some cases, from individual congressmen. Indeed, the origin of most policy proposals is so complex that it is difficult to parcel out credit (or blame). Rather than bursting like a mature Athena from the head of Zeus, a policy proposal goes through a long period of maturation. But the president possesses virtually unequalled technical resources and political visibility which give him a tremendous opportunity to define national goals and to translate those goals into specific policy proposals.

The president's role in policy initiation is now widely accepted, although this has not always been the case. Congress expects the president to provide such policy proposals. Criticism is likely to arise not because of such proposals, but because of their absence or their specific content. In 1953, for example, President Eisenhower decided not to submit a legislative program to Congress, apparently feeling it would usurp the proper functions of Congress. This failure was widely criticized. One Republican committee chairman was alleged to have told the White House:

Don't expect us to start from scratch on what you people want. That's not the way we do things here. You draft the bills and we work them over.[10]

Many commentators have suggested that in the initiation of policy proposals the president has become predominant. Some have gone further to suggest that Congress primarily ratifies what the president proposes. But congressmen do not blindly follow the wishes of the president as was evident in both the administrations of John Kennedy and Lyndon Johnson. Considerable effort has to be devoted to persuade, coerce or cajole congressmen to support presidential proposals. Congress has retained the rights to criticize, amend, add to or delay proposals. It still has the unassailable right to say "no" to presidential requests for laws or money. Presidential-congressional relations cannot be characterized by any simple superior-subordinate relationship, but are a complex pattern of conflict, compromise and cooperation. Indeed, Congress has demonstrated a remarkable capacity for survival in an age of executive ascendancy.[11]

If the president's initiation of policy is separated into those areas pertaining to domestic affairs and those areas pertaining to defense and foreign policy then some striking differences emerge.[12] In the former category, the president is less successful in having his way; his proposals are subject to alteration, modification and occasional defeat. It takes, perhaps, an unusual crisis, such as Franklin Roosevelt's hundred days in the midst of a depression or the large congressional majorities that Lyndon Johnson enjoyed, for a president to gain success in controlling domestic policy. In the category of foreign and defense policy, however, presidents have had much greater success in determining policy. In contrast to the negotiation and bargaining necessary in domestic policies, presidents since World War II have normally been able to get support for their foreign policies.

The president's formal powers to act in foreign affairs and defense are vast and difficult to restrict. Here, Congress is more likely to be confronted with an accomplished fact: support for an exile invasion of Cuba, military intervention in the Dominican Republic, escalation of a war in Southeast Asia. Most major foreign policy doctrines are known by the name of the particular president: the Monroe Doctrine, Roosevelt's "good neighbor" policy, the Truman Doctrine, the Kennedy Alliance for Progress or the Nixon Doctrine. Congress is more likely to be called upon to support such decisions rather than to participate in their actual formation. This is not to say that Congress cannot influence foreign policy decisions; the perennial battle over foreign aid authorization and appropriations is a case in point. But it appears that Congress has more influence over fairly peripheral matters, the least on major questions, such as those affecting our political survival. On one hand, a major legislative battle may erupt in the Senate over ratification of a consular treaty with the U.S.S.R., while during the 1962 confrontation with the Soviet Union over missile installations in Cuba, Congress was not even in session and did not collectively participate in the life-or-death decisions taken. In addition the congressional power to formally declare war seems of limited significance in an age of "wars of national liberation," Korean-type "police actions" and "push-button" warfare. Thus, a president is very likely to formulate and sketch in the major details of our foreign policy.

Not only do presidents play an important role in initiating policies, but, in turn, they naturally, almost inevitably, become advocates of those policies. Thus, we turn our attention to the third aspect of the president's role in policy-making— policy advocacy. As president, an individual possesses virtually unlimited ability to attract attention and secure an audience.

Almost any presidential statement or action is considered news. Even a presidential "belly-ache" will likely command front page attention and relegate other news to page two. Most presidents have discovered the truth in Theodore Roosevelt's claim that the presidency is a "bully good pulpit."

One object of a president's efforts is Congress. Since the fate of a good share of his programs, especially domestic, depends on Congress, he will take a strong hand in stimulating and prodding favorable actions—what he considers favorable. A stream of messages and other communications flows almost unceasingly between the White House and Capitol Hill. Presidential aides will spend a good deal of time cultivating friends and allies in the two legislative chambers. And at times the president may try to persuade indirectly by attempting to rally public opinion to his side, as Franklin Roosevelt did in his famous "fireside chats" on radio. Today a nationally televised presidential press conference, in the hands of a skillful practitioner, may serve the same purpose. Thus, there are a variety of tools available to the president in his legislative campaigns.

Another object of his persuasive efforts is the administration. For in controlling the bureaucracy a president cannot rely solely on formal authority; rather his control may be more dependent on his ability to convince his subordinates of the wisdom or, at least, desirability of his policies. As one astute commentator on the presidency put it: "Powers are no guarantee of power . . . presidential power is the power to persuade." [13] President Harry S. Truman said almost the same thing: "I sit here all day trying to persuade people to do the things they ought to have sense to do without my persuading them. . . . That's all the powers of the President amount to." [14] Many presidents have quickly discovered that within the maze of the bureaucracy many a plan or order is subtly sabotaged and many a presidential wish frustrated. He discovers that many agencies do not have his priorities and concerns and may feel more accountable to powerful figures on Capitol Hill and the clientele they serve than to him. Indeed, in the president's relations with the bureaucracy we see an interesting example of what Louis Koenig called the "imagined presidency" and the "real presidency." [15] As Koenig points out, the presidency is vested in our minds with more power than it really has: As a result of the pomp and ceremony surrounding it, the prestige derived from its past and the aura around some of its past occupants, we assume that a president can do more than he really can. "The real presidency is what the presidency effectively is in the present, what it can do in a given situation." [16] And in regard to the administration what a president can do may depend more on his ability to persuade than to command.

Another object of presidential persuasive efforts is the public itself. For a president knows, or soon learns, that the success or failure of his policies may rest with the public, or at least with specialized sub-publics within the general public. Perhaps, he can translate public support into pressure upon recalcitrant legislators or administrators. Or such a base of support can lead to voluntary compliance with and acceptance of policies that might otherwise be delayed, impeded or destroyed by public apathy or hostility.

Presidents have used their "bully good pulpit" not only to win support for their immediate policies, but also to educate with longer range goals in mind. Shortly before his assassination, President John Kennedy began an educational effort in the area of foreign policy. He was emphasizing the themes of cooperation and accommodation in our relations with the Soviet Union, rather than the "cold war" themes of conflict and competition. Many wished President Johnson had used the Kerner report on the growing racial chasm in America as the basis of an educational effort rather than largely ignoring a major social document.

In regard to such use of the presidency, Theodore Roosevelt bluntly commented: "I did not divine how the people were going to think; I simply made up my mind what they ought to think, and then did my best to get them to think it." [17] Although few would be so candid, many presidents have attempted this. And a president has tremendous potential, because of the great visibility of his office and its prestige and tradition, to provide public support for the political system for broad courses of action and specific policies. Success, however, is not assured simply because of the presidential seal of approval, but it is a major weapon in his quest for popular approval.

☆

THE PRESIDENT AS A PARTY LEADER

The preceding enumeration of presidential functions has omitted discussion of the president as a party leader. For the president is not only a national leader—a leader of all, above the tumult of petty squabbles and partisan bickering—he is also a partisan leader enmeshed in electioneering, fund-raising and patronage. As such, he is expected, in the venerable phrase, to "point with pride" to the record and achievements of his own party and its candidates and to "view with alarm" the opposition.

This partisan role exists in a state of more or less continuous tension with his broader leadership responsibilities and, indeed, at times may openly conflict with it. This is especially so because as a party leader, the president is "an uncertain monarch of a loose and far-flung party empire of several satrapies and dependencies and a host of self-governing commonwealths. His sway is full over a few parts; over most, it is nonexistent." [18] Thus, while party may serve fairly well as a vehicle to unite a president and his fellow partisans temporarily in the common quest for office; it does not serve as a dependable vehicle for the implementation of programs and promises into policies. Once in power, many of the president's fellow partisans may treat his program in a very cavalier fashion. Rather than receiving their automatic support, he may be compelled to negotiate, bargain and cajole for it. Indeed, he may have to turn to the opposition to receive enough support to achieve his policies. Thus, the partisanship of the campaign trail is muted because of the frequent necessity to construct bipartisan policy coalitions. While a few presidents, endowed with considerable party skill or favored by rather extraordinary events or circumstances, have had considerable success as a party leader, most presidents in Louis Koenig's phrase have found it "hobbled by uncertainty and frailty." [19]

While a president's function as a party leader may conflict with other functions, it may also provide a foundation of support for his policies. Thus, if the president behaves in a highly partisan fashion, he may alienate potential supporters of his program in the other camp; but, at the same time, such partisanship may secure for him the support of some of his own wavering partisans. This is very characteristic of presidential functions: they are both conflicting and complementary. This characteristic is important for the occupant of the office, for while it has been said that a president plays many roles, he does not play them seriatim but simultaneously. He is not one kind of leader in the morning, another in the afternoon. Rather the roles are intermingled, not discrete. His task, and one of the tests of his skill, is the weaving of the strengths of the various roles into what Clinton Rossiter has called a "seamless unity." Thus while these conflicting demands may make his total task complex, they also add new dimensions of power to his office to the extent that he can employ influence derived from one role to justify another.

☆

THEORIES OF
PRESIDENTIAL POWER

Although a president may perform many functions, the way in which these functions are performed and the way they are related, one to another, depends on the particular incumbent. Even though the office is encrusted with tradition and custom, each occupant brings a personal dimension to the office and its functions. As Edward Corwin points out: "What the Presidency is, at any particular moment, depends in important measure on who is President." [20]

Based on an examination of the history of the presidency, Louis Koenig, a careful student of the office, has suggested three basic presidential types: the literalist, the strong and a type occupying the middle ground between the two.[21]

The best definition of a literalist president was provided by one of their number, William Howard Taft:

> The true view of the Executive function is, as I conceive it, that the President can exercise no power which cannot be fairly and reasonably traced to some specific grant of power or justly implied and included within such express grant as proper and necessary to its exercise. Such specific grant must be either in the Federal Constitution or in an act of Congress passed in pursuance thereof. There is no undefined residuum of power which he can exercise because it is the public interest. . . . The grants of executive power are necessarily in general terms in order not to embarrass the executive within the field of action plainly marked for him, but his jurisdiction must be justified and vindicated by affirmative constitutional or statutory provision or it does not exist.[22]

As Taft's statement suggests, the mark of a literalist president is close obedience to the letter of the Constitution and to the traditional separation of powers. Presidential powers are seen primarily in a negative sense, restricting and confining, rather than as a vast repository of powers enabling the president to be the main source of energy in the political system. In many ways, Congress is seen as the preeminent branch needing little guidance or direction from the president. He is, as Grant put it, "a purely administrative officer," obeying the constitutional injunction "to take care that the laws be faithfully executed."[23] As another example of this type, James Buchanan, wrote: "my duty is to execute the laws . . . and not my individual opinions."[24] Such a president also plays the political role sparingly, preferring to remain above the battle and thus emphasizing the chief of state role at the expense of some of the more political roles. He prefers to reign, rather than govern. This view of presidential power is generally held by presidents who have little taste for policy innovation or change and seems ideally suited for a proponent of the status quo. It also seems more suitable for fairly placid, normal times. Sidney Hyman sees James Buchanan as the personification of this concept, which flourished in the nineteenth century and can also be seen in the two Harrisons, Fillmore, Pierce, Grant, Garfield and Arthur. But Hyman also includes a number of twentieth-century presidents, such as Taft, Harding, Coolidge, and Hoover.

At the other end of the continuum from the literalist is what Koenig calls the strong president (or Hyman's Lincoln concept of the presidency). This interpretation is represented by Jackson, Lincoln, Wilson and the two Roosevelts. This point of view was well expressed by Theodore Roosevelt in his "stewardship theory" of the presidency:

> My belief was that it was not only his right, but his duty to do anything that the needs of the Nation demanded unless such action was forbidden by the Constitution or by the laws. . . . In other words, I acted for the public welfare, I acted for the common well-being of all our people, whenever and in whatever manner was necessary. . . .[25]

Or by Woodrow Wilson when he declared that "the President is at liberty, both in law and conscience to be as big a man as he can." [26]

Rather than interpreting his powers in a limited fashion, such a president views them with maximum liberality and, in the process, frequently incurs constitutional controversies and establishes new, and breaks old, precedents, thus enlarging the presidential role in our system. The emphasis is on the political, not the legalistic. As a result the president becomes far more than an administrative officer. As Wilson said:

> . . . they are administering it [the Presidency] in its truest purpose and with greatest effect by regarding themselves as less and less executive officers and more and more directors of affairs and leaders of the nation. . . .[27]

Or as Franklin Roosevelt wrote: "The Presidency is not merely an administrative office. It is pre-eminently a place of moral leadership." [28]

A more recent president, John F. Kennedy, said almost the same thing in different words: "We need instead what the Constitution envisioned: a Chief Executive who is the vital center of action in our whole scheme of government." [29] He must be, in Kennedy's words,

. . . a vigorous proponent of the national interest—not a passive broker for conflicting private interests. They demand a man capable of acting as the commander-in-chief of the grand alliance, not merely a bookkeeper who feels that his work is done when the numbers on the balance sheet come out even. They demand that he be the head of a responsible party, not rise so far above politics as to be invisible—a man who will formulate and fight for legislative politics, not be a casual bystander to the legislative process.[30]

Bent on change and innovation, such a president becomes the central point of leadership in the political system.

The third type—Koenig's "middle ground" type or Hyman's Cleveland concept—shuttles somewhat between the other two. One time it emphasizes the purely administrative aspects of the presidency; at other times, broader dimensions of the office. At one time, it defers to Congress; subsequently, it is pushing and prodding Congress. Its distinctive trait is that it views the essential presidential functions in a defensive direction: use of executive energy and weapons (such as the veto) to maintain an existing equilibrium. Examples of this type include the presidencies of the two Adamses, Van Buren, Andrew Johnson, Hayes and Cleveland. The presidency of Eisenhower might also fall into this category.[31] Philosophically inclined to the literalist view, Eisenhower found, with the passage of time, that the literalist view was too limiting, that the modern presidency had to be unshackled. Thus, the gravitational center of the Eisenhower concept in practice was the Cleveland concept: the president does not lead; he vetoes and stops "bad" things which others start.

Both Koenig and Hyman suggest that no matter how adequate such concepts as the literalist or the middle ground may have been in the past, they are not adequate in the modern world. Rather the demands of our domestic problems and our world responsibilities require a presidency that is continuously strong. And our task, they suggest, may be not to limit the presidency as to convert it from an office that is only intermittently strong into one that is continuously strong.[32]

But even if all presidents adhere to the "strong" type, presidents differ in and are limited by their own political skills and abilities, their own personalities and their vision and goals.[33] Thus, this personal dimension would affect their performance even if they all shared the concept of a strong president. And such a president may not emerge unless some sort of political and social consensus exists which will sustain a major confrontation with public problems. While he may have a role in creating such a consensus, the political and social environment also circumscribes his behavior as president.

☆

SOURCES OF PRESIDENTIAL POWER

Any president has at his disposal a wide array of powers. For convenience they can be divided into three major categories: constitutional, statutory and extraconstitutional.[34]

The first category consists of power vested in the president by the basic law—the Constitution—and exercisable by him on his own initiative. For example, he is assigned powers pertaining to the executive branch of government. Article II declares that "the executive power shall be vested in a President of the United States." Another clause tells him to "take care that the laws be faithfully executed." Three provisions pertain to his powers in relation to the legislative branch: a) the power to convene or adjourn Congress under certain circumstances, b) the veto power over legislation, and c) the power to send messages to Congress recommending measures, such as the traditional "state of the Union" message. The president is also given vast powers in foreign affairs and national defense, such as the power to receive ambassadors, negotiate treaties, be commander-in-chief of the armed forces. He is also given the power to grant pardons and reprieves to those convicted of federal offenses.

The powers which flow from the Constitution, either directly or by deduction from it, make an impressive array even in the hands of a president with a limited conception of the office. But in the hands of a strong president, they take on very broad dimensions and arouse raging national debates over the extent of such powers. The vague language with which they are phrased invites a struggle between an activist president and those who oppose him and his policies. Amid cries of "dictatorship," such critics take him to task for violating the Constitution and usurping the prerogatives of other branches. They attempt to circumscribe his powers as much as possible. On the other hand, such an activist president interprets his powers with maximum liberality, defending his actions as being fully in accord with the Constitution.

Much of a president's authority is delegated to him by statute to enable him to create national policies. Covering a wide array of topics, ranging from organization of the executive branch to tariffs and from labor-management relations to natural resources policy, such authority reflects the variety of functions and services of the modern welfare state. Such powers, like his constitutional powers, are frequently granted in very broad language and confer upon him considerable discretion in implementing policies. The complexity of modern government also means that many of these powers are not so much exercised by the president directly as they are exercised by his subordinates in his name.

An excellent example of the legislative contribution to the expansion of presidential power is the legislature's transfer of some of its budgetary powers to him. Through the Budget and Accounting Act of 1921, a centralized executive budget was established, and the agency—the Bureau of the Budget—created to prepare such a document has become a major legislative and management tool for the president. Although Congress, and particularly the appropriations committees, retains the right to reject requests, the basic plan from which they work is an executive document, and the fact that this bill became law during the tenure of Warren Harding suggests that a strong presidency is to a considerable degree a consequence of a changing political environment and not entirely who is president.

A third kind of presidential power is extraconstitutional—what Hirschfield calls "the American manifestation of that executive authority which John Locke defined as the power to act 'according to discretion for the public good, without the prescription of the law and sometimes even against it.' " [35] This kind of power, frequently denied in theory and jurisprudence, has been resorted to by almost every leader in a crisis. The best example is Abraham Lincoln as evidenced by some of his actions during the Civil War—unauthorized expenditures of public funds, independent raising of an army, etc. When such actions were criticized and condemned, Lincoln responded in very candid terms:

I did understand, however, that my oath to preserve the Constitution to the best of my ability, imposed on me the duty of preserving, by every indispensable means that government—that nation—of which the Constitution was the organic law. Was it possible to lose a nation and yet preserve the Constitution? . . . I felt that measures, otherwise unconstitutional, might become lawful, by becoming indispensable to the preservation of the Constitution, through the preservation of the nation.[36]

But other examples could be cited, for presidents have in fact exceeded their legal and constitutional authority in almost every instance of national emergency. When Franklin D. Roosevelt in the depths of a devastating depression closed the banks, or in the early days of World War II interned citizens of Japanese ancestry, or when Harry S. Truman responded in Korea, to what he regarded as a major Communist challenge, and so committed the nation to war on his own initiative, they were acting in the Lincoln tradition. Such a tradition is at the core of the modern presidency and has in numerous instances been legitimized through public approval: that the president as a "Popular Tribune" is the "sole repre-

sentative of all the people" and possesses great power to preserve and protect the nation. Or as Woodrow Wilson wrote:

His is the only national voice in affairs. Let him once win the ad-
miration and confidence of the country and no other single force can
withstand him, no combination of forces can easily overpower
him. His position takes the imagination of the country. He is the
representative of no constituency, but of the whole people.[37]

With strong, popular backing, a skillful president, in times of
crisis or national concern can push his powers to the limits
of constitutionality and perhaps even beyond. For in times
of crisis, the presidency as a symbol of unity and instrument
of action is where the nation turns for leadership. Thus, as
Hirschfield concludes, "the needs of the nation and the support
of its citizens are the real sources of Presidential power, un-
locking all the authority in the Constitution and the laws,
as well as availing the executive of powers which go beyond
the broadest interpretation of that prodigious combination." [38]

Such popular support is of two types: first, general public
backing for a specific policy or policies, although such general
support occurs infrequently. It takes a sense of urgency, such
as that which sustained Franklin Roosevelt during the legend-
ary first hundred days of the New Deal, as a nation severely
wounded by the Depression cast about for hope and a reversal
of its fortunes. Or the type of national climate that prevailed
and buttressed John F. Kennedy during the tense confrontation of the Cuban missile crisis. On the other hand, the absence of such general support—and indeed, the existence of
serious divisions within the public, such as developed during
the course of the Korean War or the conflict in South Vietnam—can impose serious limitations on the actions of a president.

The other type of support is not so much approval for a
specific policy as it is a widespread mood of confidence in the
president as an individual. This more subtle evaluation is
based on intangibles difficult to measure precisely, such as his
leadership qualities—a general impression of who is in charge
—and his "style." Koenig defines style as a "cumulative, more

or less representative impression inferred from . . . elements of conduct." [39] These elements include, among others, his gestures and flairs, his oral and written communications, his interests, enthusiasms and prejudices. Such public approval, of course, does not guarantee success. A case in point was John F. Kennedy, who, despite a high popular standing, had difficulty translating campaign promises into policies. But it is a major asset which, especially if the times are ripe, can be used by a skillful practitioner to expand presidential power.

☆
THE CHANGING PRESIDENCY

When Richard Nixon took the presidential oath in January 1969, he was assuming an office encrusted with custom and tradition and a depository of vast powers and diverse expectations. But he was also assuming an office that differed very significantly from the one envisioned by those who founded it. The presidency rather than having its character irrevocably fixed by the Constitution, like other political institutions, has been altered under the pressure of events and the men who occupied the office. Edward Corwin suggests that the history of the presidency has been one of aggrandizement, but it has not been a uniformly continuous trend. Forward surges have been followed by retreats and limitations.[40] But the overall trend remains clear: enhancement of the power and influence of the office.

There are a number of factors that have influenced the development of the executive. These include: 1) broadening the popular base of the government, 2) ambiguity in the constitutional phrases defining presidential power and duties, 3) the expansion of the role of government, 4) recurring periods of emergency and peril, and 5) the rise of the United States as a major world power.

An important factor in the development of the presidency has been the democratization of the means of nominating and electing the chief executive. It lends substance to the claim that he is the only official elected by all the people, and, thus able to rise above parochial concerns and interests and represent the "public interest." Claims of a broad-based popular mandate may also enable him to maximize his persuasive powers with other policy-makers, such as Congress.

Another important factor is the ambiguity in the constitutional provisions defining his power and duties, noted earlier. Rather than being precise and restrictive, the language is imprecise and broad. Because of this ambiguity a particular incumbent's conception of his role, and his skill and daring in discharging it, become key elements in giving substance to the executive function. Such ambiguity is also an open invitation to disagreement and controversy. Thus both a strong, bold president and his opponents, critical of his use of power, may cite the Constitution to defend their respective positions.

The role of the chief executive has also been profoundly altered by the economic and social changes in the nation. As a concomitant to these changes, such as industrialization and urbanization, there has been a popular demand for the government to assume new regulative and service functions, to move from the narrow policeman's function, which was defined as the role of government in a society under the sway of laissez-faire doctrines, to providing the full array of services and functions encompassed under the label of the "welfare state." Not only are the new demands more numerous in number and scope, but they also differ in kind from earlier ones. They require a high degree of technical knowledge and skill, appear and change rapidly and necessitate continuous, rather than sporadic, attention. Nor do such policies stand alone, as discrete items, as they frequently did in the nineteenth century. Rather, they are closely interrelated to meet the needs of a functionally interdependent society. The responsibility for the government's direction and supervision has fallen more heavily on the executive than any other branch. Although the legislative branch has considerable responsibility, it has increasingly delegated vast discretionary authority to the executive. The president is also expected to interject energy and direction into the vast bureaucratic complex set up to implement such programs and to provide planning and coordination. In addition, he is expected to take the initiative in proposing new programs or expansion of existing ones. Indeed part of his reputation as an effective president may depend upon his success in originating and obtaining legislative approval for new social programs.

Executive power seems to thrive and expand under conditions of crisis. And one of the characteristics of our modern age is that we seem to live in a state of perpetual crisis—the Depression of the 1930s was followed by World War II, which, in turn, was followed after a brief interval by the Korean War. Whether the crisis is a war (declared or undeclared), the threat of one, severe economic distress, natural disasters or civil disturbances, people seem to turn almost inexorably to the executive. And other branches may defer at least temporarily to his judgments and decisions, even when his actions seem to treat them in a highly cavalier fashion. They reserve their retribution for more tranquil times. Thus, the height of executive powers under Lincoln was followed by the attempt of Congress to virtually subjugate the president to the legislative will. But it is noteworthy as Joseph Kallenback points out that such executive claims offered and successfully utilized in one crisis become the benchmarks from which new claims of executive authority are made in the next emergency.[41]

Finally, the rise of the United States to the role of a world power and the extent to which foreign affairs has dominated the arena of public affairs has had a profound effect on the presidency.[42] For in these areas, the president has long-standing advantages over the other branches—unity, secrecy and dispatch in decision-making are frequently cited.

As we pointed out earlier, we have, in effect, two presidencies: one for domestic affairs and one for foreign affairs and national defense. And it is in the latter area that presidential power and influence is most potent. Indeed, in a day of "push-button" warfare, "hot-lines" and weapons of ultimate destruction, such power is staggering.[43] The major role of the president in foreign affairs has also enlarged his constituency to include the leaders and people of other lands. While they have no direct voice in his election, they observe his actions with keen interest and attempt in diverse ways to influence his actions and policies.

☆

THE INSTITUTIONALIZED PRESIDENCY

As the preceding discussion has suggested, the presidency is a position of extraordinary powers and responsibilities. To help the occupant perform his duties, a number of offices and councils have been established. Indeed, Louis Koenig has suggested that it is helpful to think of the presidency not as one man, but as a series of concentric rings, with the president in the center and the various rings representing councils or advisers, each one more distant from the president and less significant in presidential decision-making.[44]

Such staff assistance can help the president in a number of ways, including the gathering of information for him either on a specific problem or agency.[45] On a longer term basis, presidential staffs can analyze and prepare proposals for future programs and policies. They can represent the president in various committees and meetings. After a presidential order has been issued, they can check to see if it has been implemented. Another function is that of serving as a buffer absorbing as many complaints as possible and screening people who want to see the President. They may also supervise a great number of agencies for him, alerting him to possible problems and dangers. And, on occasion, they can serve as scapegoats, shouldering the blame when something goes wrong. Their dismissal may relieve some of the pressures and placate some of the antagonized groups.

This development of the presidential staff is a fairly recent innovation.[46] As late as 1933, when Franklin D. Roosevelt entered the White House confronted by great problems and challenges, there was only a very rudimentary staff—three professional staff members, three secretaries (press, appointments, corresponding) and a small clerical staff. Roosevelt frequently coopted staff members from other agencies, in some cases moving them directly into the White House. He also relied on a number of old friends, such as Judge Samuel Rosenman. Recognizing the need for additional staff assistance, Roosevelt set up the President's Committee on Administrative Management, chaired by Louis Brownlow, whose report in 1937 led to a major reorganization and expansion of presidential staff. Today the president is surrounded by a growing host of advisers, councils and offices. Thus, the problem now is to establish some sort of balance between staff sufficient to enable the president to perform his duties and a staff that is not so large and complex as to dominate or isolate the president.

Each president must strike his own balance, develop his own pattern of decision-making. One type, illustrated by the Eisenhower presidency, is a hierarchical structure. Somewhat on the order of a military chain of command, it emphasized formal mechanisms, such as committees, specialization and clearly defined access to the president through a hierarchy of aides. At the top of the command, just below the president, was Sherman Adams, functioning as a chief of staff controlling all access to and, at least in domestic matters, most proposals or information reaching the president. Another type of arrangement, illustrated by Roosevelt, is a very personal and flexible one—a form of almost "creative chaos." Lacking a real chain of command, staff members had individual access to the president, were personally supervised by the president and frequently duplicated each other's assignments by conscious design of the president who ignored specialization. Eschewing formal devices, Roosevelt relied heavily on a number of troubleshooters such as Harry Hopkins, who, disdainful of jurisdictional boundaries and specialization, acted as the eyes and ears for the president. Both Kennedy and Johnson came closer to the Roosevelt model than to the Eisenhower model, preferring to act as their own chief of staff. Each staff organization, even while bearing elements of the past, obviously reflects to a considerable extent the personal style, temperament and methods of operating of a particular incumbent.[47]

Among the staff facilities and councils that have grown up around the president are the following:

a) The White House Office

Each president has his own personal staff, including a variety of special assistants for press relations, liaison with Congress, speechwriting, patronage, national security matters, etc. Its essence is its personal nature, consisting of persons whom the president trusts and are strictly accountable to him, who are closely attuned to his style and manner.

b) The Office of Management and Budget (formerly the Bureau of the Budget)

This is a more specialized and permanent agency in character. Most of its staff members continue regardless of who is president. It not only prepares the annual budget, in itself a tremendous undertaking in a day of astronomical spending programs, but it also serves in a supervision-coordination role, clearing new legislative proposals before they are sent to Congress and reviewing the management and organization of federal agencies.

c) The Council of Economic Advisers

This council consists of professional economists who advise the president on the current state of the economy as well as recommending ways of keeping the economy healthy.

d) The National Security Council

This advisory group was created by the National Security Act of 1947 to advise the president on how to coordinate domestic, foreign and military policy. Among its permanent members are the president, the vice-president, the secretary of State and the secretary of Defense. Others such as the director of the Central Intelligence Agency and the chairman of the Joint Chiefs of Staff frequently take part. The extent to which presidents have relied on it has varied considerably. Eisenhower met with it frequently; Kennedy, however, preferred to rely on small *ad hoc* groups.

There are also a number of other units in the Executive Office, such as the Office of Science and Technology, Office for Emergency Planning (responsible for preparing for mobilization of the nation's resources in event of war or natural disaster) and the National Aeronautics and Space Council. To add to the list, President Nixon created a Domestic Council. Consisting of all cabinet members, except the secretaries of State and Defense, it is designed to tie together interagency planning in the domestic field, a domestic counterpart of the National Security Council. In addition, Congress as part of the National Environmental Policy Act created a White House Council on Environmental Quality.

During any administration there are also generally a number of informal advisers and confidants who remain in private life but are called upon by the president to be participants in the policy-making process. For example, during the Johnson administration, both Abe Fortas, an influential Washington lawyer (who later served for a while on the Supreme Court) and Clark Clifford, also a Washington lawyer (who served briefly as secretary of Defense) were frequently consulted by the president.

In any administration there is usually an "inner circle" (what in Andrew Jackon's time was called a "kitchen cabinet") —that is, a small group of men who regardless of position are very close to the president and involved in major decisions. A good example in the early Nixon administration was Attorney General John Mitchell. As a result of his past association with the president—law partner and campaign manager—Nixon consulted him on a wide variety of issues ranging from Vietnam policy to welfare policy and campus disorders.

Institutionalization, however, in many ways is a mixed blessing. While it has provided definite benefits to the contemporary president, there are problems as well. There is the danger of isolating the president so that he is closed off from all but his staff. Presidential aides, attuned to his style and thoughts, may become simply "yes" men, fearing that negative thoughts or challenges to presidential thinking may imperil their standing and career. Another problem is the relationship between such aides and other governmental officials, particularly the cabinet officers. Rather than simply checking on agency activities, presidential aides may assume almost operational direction of a department creating problems of rivalry and duplication.[47] As the staff aides increase in number, the president must spend more and more time giving guidance and direction to them. His staff may become objects of attack by groups who hope in this way to injure the president (for example, Sherman Adams for Eisenhower or Walter Jenkins for Johnson). Because of the increased attention given to presidential aides by the media, they frequently become public figures in their own right. Their public posture and concern with their own image may reduce their effectiveness as advisers and lead to jealousy and attempts to secure additional publicity.

While such advice and assistance is essential for any president, its value and usefulness will depend ultimately on the particular president—his capacity to attract able advisers, the qualities of direction and inspiration that he supplies to them and the uses he makes of them.

This review of the powers and functions of the president suggests the executive's central position in the governmental structure. The office, while retaining ties to the past, has come a long way from its origins. Once an object of suspicion and considerable hostility, it has evolved into one of the most powerful and respected positions in the world. But powerful as he is, the president is also surrounded by limitations. While he may dominate, he does not dictate.

☆

THE VICE-PRESIDENCY

It's like being naked in the middle of a blizzard, with no one to even offer you a match to help you keep warm—that's the Vice-

Presidency. You are trapped, vulnerable and alone and it does not matter who happens to be President.

Hubert H. Humphrey[48]

In considering the modern presidency, one must also examine the position of vice-president. This office has a very mixed historical record.[49] In the early years of the republic the office was held by distinguished public figures—first John Adams and then Thomas Jefferson, both of whom truly could be called the second citizens of the nation and who subsequently went on to become president as well. But in the nineteenth century, the office rapidly faded into obscurity and the prominence of the men selected to hold the office also declined. In 1868, Gideon Welles suggested it was an office "without responsibility, patronage or any duty worthy of honorable aspiration." [50] Before 1900, no vice-president was nominated to continue in office. Also, before 1900, no vice-president who succeeded to the office through the death of the President—Tyler, Fillmore, Johnson and Arthur—was nominated for his own elected term as president. Although there were occasional men of prominence in the office, such as John C. Calhoun, most like Daniel Tompkins, Richard Johnson and Henry Wilson have sunk into oblivion.

Occasionally there was a flurry of interest in the office and particularly the man holding it when something happened to the president. In this century four men have died in office— William McKinley, Warren Harding, Franklin Roosevelt and John Kennedy. Two presidents, Wilson and Eisenhower, suffered severe illnesses and for a time could not perform their duties. Prior to this century several presidents were assassinated, Lincoln and Garfield, and two, William H. Harrison and Zachary Taylor, met natural deaths while in office. Although such dramatic and often tragic events should have created and sustained interest in the vice-presidency, such interest was short-lived and rapidly eroded.

In recent years, however, the office has taken on a new look and importance. The main reason for the heightened stature of vice-presidents is the deliberate efforts made by recent presidents to give additional duties to this office. Because of their heavy and increased responsibilities and numerous functions, presidents have looked to their vice-presidents for help. Today, it is no longer true as one wag put it in the 1890s that the vice-president has "nothing on his mind except the health of the President." [51] During President Roosevelt's first term, Vice-President John Nance Garner helped put the New Deal's legislative program through Congress. Henry Wallace, who served during Roosevelt's third term took on some executive functions, such as the chairmanship of the Board of Economic Warfare during World War II, although without great success. In 1949, the vice-president was made a statutory member of the newly created National Security Council. During the Eisenhower presidency, his vice-president for both terms, Richard Nixon, was one of the most publicized occupants in the history of that office. And he performed a number of tasks for Eisenhower especially of a ceremonial and political character. He also assumed additional executive responsibilities, such as chairing a Committee on Government Contracts. Both Lyndon B. Johnson and Hubert Humphrey as vice-presidents performed rather similar functions.[52]

The functions performed by the modern vice-president fall into a number of categories:

a) ceremonial

These are akin to those performed by the president as chief of state and, indeed, frequently the vice-president is a stand-in for the president. Such duties have also generally involved traveling abroad. As vice-president, Lyndon Johnson made eleven foreign tours in less than three years. For example, in 1961, after the construction of the Berlin Wall by East Germany, Johnson went to show the flag and to bolster the spirit of a beleaguered city.

b) legislative

Here the vice-president has certain constitutional functions such as presiding over the Senate and voting in case of a tie. In addition, some vice-presidents, particularly those with previous legislative service, attempt to exert behind-the-scenes influence in support of the president's legislative program. A good example was Hubert Humphrey as vice-president.

c) executive

These assignments for the vice-president have continued to accumulate. Thus, the vice-president, as mentioned earlier, is a statutory member of the National Security Council and chairs the Space Council. Both Vice-Presidents Humphrey and Agnew provided White House liaison with the nation's mayors. Indeed, Professor Paul David has concluded that the vice-presidency is in transition to a new institutional status as an office predominantly in the executive while retaining its constitutional prerogatives in the legislature.[53] While such executive functions cannot be expanded or enlarged except through at least the tacit consent of the president, once such functions have been established, withdrawal may be fairly difficult.

d) party or partisan activities

Vice-presidents increasingly have assumed some of the burdens of party leader, particularly in campaigning for the party's candidates at the state and local level, engaging in fund-raising activities, etc. For example, Eisenhower was disinclined to play much of a partisan role. Thus, much of this activity, especially campaigning in mid-term elections, fell on Nixon. The political credits he compiled as a result of such activities paid off in both 1960 and 1968 in his two successful bids for his party's presidential nomination. Even a more partisan president may at times prefer to eschew partisan activity, preferring to delegate it to a political "hatchet man," such as the vice-president. Thus, in the early Nixon administration, the president urged Americans to unite and "lower their voices," while Vice-President Agnew made strident attacks upon the president's critics, thus compounding the turmoil and confusion.

After a careful assessment of the development of the office, Paul David concluded that future vice-presidents can be routinely expected to serve as deputy chiefs of state and deputy party leaders, to also assist the president in the field of foreign affairs, to continue to accumulate executive functions and to receive *ad hoc* legislative assignments. He also suggests that the vice-president is rapidly achieving a status in which he will be one of the most likely presidential nominees of his party when the president is unavailable. Finally, he suggests that despite its new duties and prominence, the vice-presidency still is a "second man position" characterized by considerable ambiguity, a degree of psychological insecurity and requiring a measure of personal self-denial.[54]

NOTES

1. Quoted in Arthur B. Tourtellot, *Presidents on the Presidency* (Garden City, N.Y.: Doubleday and Co., 1964), p. 366.

2. Ibid., p. 363.

3. Ibid., p. 370.

4. Richard Neustadt, "The Reality of Presidential Power," *The Power of the Presidency*, ed., Robert S. Hirschfield (New York: Atherton Press, 1968), p. 273.

5. For somewhat different categories of presidential roles, see Clinton Rossiter, *The American Presidency* (New York: Harcourt Brace and World, Inc., 1960), pp. 15–43. Also Louis Brownlow, *The President and the Presidency* (Chicago: Public Administration Service, 1949), pp. 52–72.

6. For an analysis of the president's symbolic role, see Fred I. Greenstein, "Psychological Functions of the President for Citizens," *The American Presidency: Vital Center*, ed. Elmer Cornwell, Jr. (Glenview, Ill.: Scott, Foresman and Co., 1966), pp. 30–36. This section draws heavily from his perceptive analysis. For some dangers of this symbolic role to the president, see George E. Reedy, *The Twilight of the Presidency* (New York: World Publishing Co., 1970), especially Chapter 1. Also see Thomas E. Cronin, "Superman, Our Textbook President," *Washington Monthly*, October 1970, 47–54.

7. Note the very personal reactions of many Americans to the loss of a president—the Kennedy assassination. A report on such reaction based on a national study is found in the New York *Times*, March 7, 1964.

8. Tourtellot, p. 59.

9. Ibid., p. 122.

10. Related in Richard Neustadt, "The Presidency and Legislation: Planning the President's Program," *American Political Science Review*, December 1955, 1015.

11. For a discussion of the modern roles and functions of Congress, see Dale Vinyard, *Congress* (New York: Charles Scribner's Sons, 1968), Chapter 1.

12. See such an analysis in Aaron Wildavsky, "The Two Presidencies," *Transaction*, December 1966, 7–14.

13. See Richard Neustadt, *Presidential Power* (New York: John Wiley & Son, 1960), p. 10.

14. Ibid., pp. 9–10.

15. See the discussion in Louis Koenig's very readable and entertaining *The Chief Executive*, rev. ed. (New York: Harcourt, Brace and World, Inc., 1968), pp. 3–8.

16. Ibid., p. 3.

17. Sidney Warren, "How Powerful is the Presidency," *The Dynamics of the American Presidency*, eds. Donald B. Johnson and Jack L. Walker (New York: John Wiley & Son, 1964), p. 301.

18. Koenig, p. 89.

19. Ibid., p. 85.

20. See Edward S. Corwin, *The President: Office and Powers*, 4th ed. (New York: New York University Press, 1957), p. 30.

21. See Koenig, pp. 10–12. Also Sidney Hyman "What is the President's True Role," Johnson and Walker, pp. 132–135. For a somewhat different classification, see James MacGregor Burns. *Presidential Government* (New York: Avon Books, 1965).

22. William Howard Taft, "Our Chief Magistrate and His Powers," Johnson and Walker, p. 137.

23. Quoted by Hyman, p. 133.

24. Quoted in Koenig, p. 10.

25. Reprinted in Hirschfield, pp. 82–84.

26. Woodrow Wilson, "Constitutional Government in the United States, Ibid., p. 93.

27. Ibid., p. 100.

28. From a 1932 speech quoted in Joseph E. Kallenback, *The American Chief Executive* (New York: Harper and Row, Inc., 1966), p. 253.

29. John F. Kennedy, Speech to the National Press Club (January 14, 1960), reprinted in Hirschfield, p. 131. For a statement of the views of Richard M. Nixon, see the text of a radio address reprinted in the New York *Times*, September 20, 1968, 33.

30. Kennedy, reprinted in Hirschfield, p. 129.

31. Hyman, pp. 134–135.

32. For a rating of the presidents by historians, see Arthur Schlesinger, Sr. "Our Presidents: A Rating by Seventy-Five Historians," The New York *Times Magazine*, July 29, 1962, 11. Also see Curtis Amlund, "President-Ranking: a Criticism," *Midwest Journal of Political Science*, August 1964, 309–15.

33. For some discussion of a much-neglected topic, personalities of presidents, see James David Barber, "Analyzing Presidents: From Passive Positive (Taft) to Active Negative (Nixon)," *Washington Monthly*, October 1969, 33–54.

34. This analysis borrows heavily from that of Hirschfield, "The Power of the Contemporary President," Hirschfield, pp. 238–55.

35. Hirschfield, pp. 241–42.

36. Lincoln's letter to A. G. Hodges, reprinted in Hirschfield, pp. 79–81.

37. Ibid., p. 243.

38. Ibid., p. 245.

39. Koenig, p. 337.

40. Corwin, pp. 29–30.

41. See Kallenback, p. 250.

42. See Sidney Warren, *The President as a World Leader* (Philadelphia: J. B. Lippincott Co., 1964). For a discussion of the role of Congress in foreign policy, see Robert A. Dahl, *Congress and Foreign Policy* (New York: Harcourt, Brace and World, Inc., 1950) and James A. Robinson, *Congress and Foreign Policy-Making* (Homewood, Ill.: The Dorsey Press, 1962).

43. For a graphic inside account of presidential decision-making in a period of great international crisis, see Robert F. Kennedy, *Thirteen Days: A Memoir of the Cuban Missile Crisis* (New York: W. W. Norton and Co., 1969).

44. See Louis Koenig, *The Invisible Presidency* (New York: Holt, Rinehart and Winston, Inc., 1960).

45. For an interesting discussion, see "The White House Staff vs. The Cabinet: Hugh Sidney Interviews Bill Moyers," *Washington Monthly*, February 1969, 3. For some discussion of internal staff politics and problems, see Reedy.

46. For an account of this development, see Alex B. Lacy, Jr., "The White House Staff Bureaucracy," *Transaction*, January 1969, 50–56.

47. For an attempt to analyze President Nixon's approach to staff, see the column by Rowland Evans and Robert Novak, Washington *Post*, January 6, 1969, editorial page, and William S. White, ibid., January 18, 1969.

48. Quoted in *Time*, November 14, 1969, 19.

49. This section relies heavily on Paul T. David, "The Vice Presidency: Its Institutional Evolution and Contemporary Status," *Journal of Politics*, November 1967, 721–48 and James MacGregor Burns, "A New Look at the Vice-Presidency," Johnson and Walker, pp. 261–65. Also see Irving G. Williams, *The Rise of the Vice-Presidency* (Washington, D.C.: Public Affairs Press, 1956).

50. Quoted in Johnson and Walker, p. 262.

51. Ibid., p. 261.

52. For an early assessment of the functions of Vice-President Spiro Agnew, see *Newsweek*, November 17, 1969, 35–42 and *Time*, November 14, 1969, 17–22.

53. David, p. 721.

54. For a summation of David's conclusions, see ibid., pp. 721–22.

THE ELECTORAL
PROCESS[1]

☆☆☆☆☆

In his widely used text on American parties, the late V. O. Key delineated two different kinds of politics—the politics of getting into office and the politics of governing.[2] The selection process affects both, through its impact on who is elected and, then, how he behaves once in office. In this chapter we will be concerned with the selection process for the highest and most visible position in our political system and will examine both the formal and informal institutions and procedures that govern it.

GENERAL CHARACTERISTICS
OF THE PROCESS

First, the presidency is an elective office, the only one with the entire nation as its constituency. The development of the presidency has been in the direction of continually democratizing the election process. At first, chosen indirectly, a variety of devices have been used to involve the electorate in the selection. Through conventions, primaries for choosing delegates and reducing the role of the Electoral College, the selection process has been made more direct and popular. Further reforms, such as abolition of the electors, would make it even more direct.

Popular election of the chief executive, however, is by no means universal among political democracies. In Great Britain, the Prime Minister is chosen by the parliamentary majority party and is never voted upon by the entire nation. Rather he is first elected to a seat from a parliamentary district, such as Yorkshire, London, etc., and then is selected by his parliamentary colleagues for the office of Prime Minister. The concept of an independently elected chief executive, who during his tenure may not be a member of the legislative body is fairly uncommon among Western democracies.

The constitutional requirements for the office are minimal —thirty-five as a minimum age, natural born citizen and nine years of residency in the United States. Instead, it is the informal requirements, a combination of personal, social and political characteristics that narrows the field, making some men "available" (desirable, attractive candidates) and seriously impedes the possible candidacy of others. The concept of "availability" is not precise in content and is subject to change as the political system itself changes. It consists of the qualities that the parties believe make an attractive, appealing and hopefully a winning candidate. Such an assessment is based upon widely shared expectations within the electorate itself as to what a president should be as well as the distribution of power in presidential politics. In the past most explanations of the concept have mentioned these factors:

white
male
married with attractive family
Protestant
rural or small-town origin
Anglo-Saxon or northwestern European in ethnic background
resident of a large state
some prior governmental office, especially governor

These characteristics have some validity in terms of former presidential nominees. But some are being modified and thus these standards for future projections may be fairly limited. In 1960, John F. Kennedy, both a Catholic and an urban political figure, was not only nominated but elected. In the last three presidential elections all the presidential nominees (with the exception of third-party candidate, George Wallace in 1968) have been senators rather than governors.

Also of considerable importance are a number of other qualities: acceptability to the major groups in the party's coalition (it is inconceivable at present that the Democrats would nominate a candidate unacceptable to organized labor); ability to attract wavering groups and voters and partisans of the other camp (General Eisenhower with his charismatic appeal cutting across economic, sectional, ethnic and partisan lines was an ideal candidate for a minority party). Given the pervasiveness of the mass media, another important quality is a man's ability to project himself well under the glare of the ubiquitous and relentless TV cameras as a strong, dynamic individual. While many of these qualities pertain more to the man as a candidate than as a president, there is also a rough assessment of whether he has what it takes to measure up to the office. Thus even some supporters, as well as many critics, of the 1968 presidential candidacy of Senator Eugene McCarthy felt this somewhat inscrutable and unpredictable man was lacking in some of the qualities necessary for the presidency.

The quadrennial quest for the presidency in many ways is a focal point for American politics. It attracts a greater voter turnout than any other election. Indeed, for many Americans, observing the drama and excitement of this contest may be the extent of their interest and awareness of American politics. Voting in this election may be their major, if not only, political activity. And it is no wonder that it attracts their attention. For as one commentator put it: "The American people have evolved a process of nomination and election to that office [the presidency] that for sheer length, expense, attention and gaudy extravaganza is certainly without peer in the world." [3]

The results of the election affect the contests for other offices as well. An attractive presidential candidate not only draws voters to himself but to other candidates on the party ticket. This is the so-called "coattail" effect. One of the main reasons for this consequence is that voters generally have a better developed image of a presidential candidate than those for lesser offices. Since voters are frequently confronted with a bed sheet ballot—offices ranging from president to local drainage commissioner—their task is fairly complex, even for a well-informed voter. Voting for those on the same ticket as their favorite presidential candidate is an easy solution.

The presidential contest has another important effect on the system. It is one of the great, centralizing forces in American politics, a centripetal force against vast, decentralizing forces that exist. Presidential candidates must capture the attention of voters and mobilize the activities of political activists. They attempt to build coalitions of support that will, at least temporarily, overcome parochial and factional interests within the party and nation. They have an important impact in defining and shaping issues and concerns of the nation as well as the public image of the party whose label they bear. Given the decentralized character of the American parties, loose confederations of state and local parties, each must attempt to unite his party for campaign purposes or construct his own viable national campaign vehicle. Indeed, Frank Sorauf suggests that what is loosely called the national party is really the party of the presidential candidate.[4]

In confronting these complex tasks, presidential candidates, however, are not entirely on their own. Their task is facilitated by the increasing national focus of American politics in terms of personalities, issues and party identification. Presidential candidates have tremendous visibility as public figures. Their names are household words. An increasing number of political activists are concerned with national issues, interest and ideologies rather than local incentives of patronage and preferment. Even party identification seems to have an increasingly national focus. The campaign for the presidency plays an important role in accentuating such developing tendencies.[5]

Presidential candidates, however, are still confronted by a largely decentralized party organization. Some years ago a perceptive commentator on American politics wrote:

Decentralization of power is by all odds the most important single characteristic of the American major party; more than anything else this trait distinguishes it from all others. Indeed once this truth is understood, nearly everything else about American parties is greatly illuminated.[6]

A more recent commentator reached this conclusion:

. . . American parties are disunited, heterogeneous conglomerations of state parties and . . . they are welded into national parties even for a brief task (nominating and electing a President) only with the greatest difficulty.[7]

Although in a real sense American parties as organizations do not exist at the national level, one cannot assume that the reverse is necessarily true at the state and local level.[8] Rather there is considerable, often startling variety from state to state. In many areas, party organization is weak or even nonexistent. Well-organized, hierarchical parties do exist. The urban political machine, of the late nineteenth and early twentieth century illustrated by Tammany Hall in New York, the Hague machine in Jersey City and Boss Curley in Boston are examples. The power of Mayor Richard Daley's Democratic organization in Chicago is a contemporary example. But these big city machines are not the norm in regard to party organization at the state and local level. The other extreme is a state of virtual disorganization. The norm of American political organization is somewhere in between, but it probably lies closer to disorganization than to a cohesive political machine.[9]

This state of affairs poses particular problems for presidential candidates. The autonomy of the state and local parties means that the national leaders can do little to control their activities (or, in some cases, lack of activity). A state organization may openly oppose the party's candidate as the Byrd organization in Virginia did the candidacy of Adlai Stevenson in 1952 and 1956. Far more common, it may sit on its hands and, perhaps, lend covert support to another candidate. This was the case in regard to Hubert Humphrey in 1968 as well as Barry Goldwater in 1964. The lack of effective party organization whether at the national level or on some state levels means a candidate may have to create his own, personal campaign organization to carry on the fight. It leads to a proliferation of *ad hoc* committees and groups. The candidate may also act as a fund-raiser to provide part of the vast sums needed for modern campaigning.

While the party as an organization may be of limited usefulness to presidential candidates, the party as a label is valuable. It draws to a candidate many voters because of their traditional party loyalty, their psychological attachment to the party. Many voters do not even wait for the campaign to begin before deciding how to vote but use the party label as a guide. For numerous voters events and issues as well as candidates take on meaning because they bear a party label. As a label, party organizes the diverse and complex stimuli of the political world—a world in which a voter may be only mildly interested or even indifferent and for which he may lack any detailed knowledge or any other frame of reference. Empirical studies have demonstrated how early partisan identification takes root, how widely it is found in the population and how durable it is.[10]

But even such partisans cannot be taken for granted. For although a voter may psychologically identify with a particular party, this does not necessarily lead to overt behavior, such as voting. Since many voters regard politics as somewhat peripheral to their lives, their participation may be sporadic rather than continuous. In any election many committed partisans must be persuaded to come to the polls.

Nor are partisan allegiances fixed for all time. An attractive opposition candidate may lead some voters to stray from traditional loyalties. A war, a sharp recession, a scandal will have an effect on some partisans. Other identifications (racial, religious, socio-economic), as they become relevant to politics, may contradict long-term partisan loyalties. If a voter feels his immediate and vital interests are not being served by his traditional party, he may bolt. Some factors are transient and only temporarily disrupt traditional loyalties. Others may be enduring and may lead to a long-term change in party preference. If such changes are widespread in the electorate, they may also lead to a major realignment of political forces and the creation of a new majority party.

There is another aspect to presidential elections which makes it difficult to rely solely on traditional party loyalty. There is some indication of an increase of the number of independents in the electorate; indeed the proportion of such identifiers has risen to an all-time high.[11] Some of these independents are to be found among the young, the better educated and more affluent. Thus, a recent Gallup Poll suggested that in no other time in recent years has the college campus been more of a political no-man's land. The proportion of students who consider themselves independents has risen steadily to a current high of 52 percent.[12]

Presidential elections, because of the high level of interest generated, also draw large numbers of weak partisans and independents to the polls. Such voters are more easily shifted from one party to another. They add disproportionately to the vote for one presidential candidate—usually the winner. On the other hand, in off-year elections (when the presidency is not at stake), these less committed partisans do not turn out in large numbers and voting is dominated by traditional partisans. Thus, in such elections there is usually a decline in support for the party that had disproportionately large numbers of these less interested voters in the last presidential election.

Since not all voters are committed partisans and since partisans can occasionally stray or even change, presidential candidates are also concerned with the way voters view the parties and, particularly, the candidates. Generally voters do not bring a strong ideological or programmatic focus to the contest. Nor do they bring detailed knowledge of the policy preferences or actions of the parties or candidates. In their monumental voting study, the authors of *The American Voter* suggested four levels of conceptualization.[13]

The first level embraced all their respondents whose evaluation of candidates and parties had any suggestion of the abtract conceptions one would associate with ideology. Among these were respondents who perceived a liberal-conservative continuum, who placed themselves at some point on this continuum and evaluated parties and candidates from this position. Also included were those who made reference to the relationship between federal power and local autonomy, the fate of individualism, etc. Also included in this group were those who used one of the labels common to ideological discussion, but without supporting perceptions that the authors term "near" ideology. Despite the generosity of the authors in defining this category, only 2½ percent of their sample, were what they considered genuine ideologues and 9 percent "near" ideology.

The second level was composed of people whose comments revolved around fairly concrete group interest, what the authors term "ideology by proxy." This level included two main types: 1) some respondents perceived politics in terms of the competition of groups, with political parties and candidates arraying themselves in favor of one and opposition to another; 2) other respondents did not carry the discussion of group interest beyond the context of one group. Thus, for example, the Democrats are good for organized labor. About 42 percent of their sample fell in this category.

Their third category consisted mainly of people making an assessment of the "goodness" or the "badness" of the times and associating it with the party in power. Generally these responses consisted of vague generalities about the times. But occasionally they pertained to isolated policy measures. This group constituted 24 percent of their sample.

Finally, the fourth category (22½ percent of their sample) consisted of responses devoid of issue content. But as the authors point out while voter participation is low in this group, they accounted for about 17 percent of the voters in the presidential election under study.[14] There were three broad types of responses: 1) party-oriented responses (they identified with a particular political party but without any apparent understanding of how it differed from its rival); 2) candidate-oriented responses (they responded to his appearance, honesty, sincerity, religiousness, family, etc.); 3) responses that had no political content except to explain that the voter had no time for politics.

These characteristics of the electorate have an impact upon the presidential candidates. For example, the candidate of the majority party may place heavy stress on party, hoping to galvanize his partisans into action, at least to go to the polls to vote their traditional party allegiance. On the other hand, the candidate of the minority party will probably play down partisanship and emphasize his particular abilities and qualifications.

Also as a result of these characteristics, presidential candidates seldom orient their national campaign to concrete issues. Rather they prefer to emphasize broad, ambiguous themes. ("Let's get America moving," "You never had it so good," "It's time for a change." "A war on crime," etc.) They also emphasize personal qualities, such as integrity, vigor, experience, decisiveness. Many voters, lacking knowledge about substantive issues, prefer to react in such non-policy, candidate-oriented terms and are willing accomplices of the candidates. As a result, however, the election may not provide an explicit policy mandate for the victor. While the election may determine who is to hold power (candidates A or B), it may not really answer the question of what they are to do with power.

While voters as a whole may not be interested in the whole plethora of policy consideration, there are always some voters concerned with particular policies, whether it be veterans' benefits, tax privileges, farm subsidies, etc. Thus a number of "issue publics" exist, people who are interested in and knowledgeable about an issue and who if their concern is threatened, will vote for or against particular candidates and parties.[15] To such groups, candidates may make fairly explicit commitments. Thus, in 1968, the Republican vice-presidential candidate, Spiro Agnew, while campaigning in oil-producing areas such as Texas, made it clear that the tax privileges of that industry would be protected by a Republican administration.

With these general comments, we will turn to an examination of the different stages in the selection process:

a) nomination: pre-convention and during convention
b) election: campaign and decision

THE NOMINATING PROCESS[16]

The process by which the parties select their presidential candidates takes place in one of two settings. In some cases the party already has a national leader—an incumbent president who has previously been elected to the office or succeeded to it. All twentieth-century chief executives who sought renomination have received it. The reasons are not difficult to understand. An incumbent has some very great advantages over challengers. The vast resources of the presidential office including its prestige and its tremendous potential for generating publicity are his. He probably also has control of the convention machinery. And finally, for a party to reject its own man would be a campaign liability, an albatross around the neck of the party nominee.

But in other cases, particularly that of the out party or where a president steps down (Lyndon Johnson in 1968), a decision must be made among a number of possible contenders.

PRE-CONVENTION

In such cases, it is hard to say just when the nominating process begins. Senator John F. Kennedy began his efforts for the 1960 Democratic presidential nomination shortly after the

1956 convention where he was defeated on the floor for his party's vice-presidential nomination. Supporters of Arizona Senator Barry Goldwater began in late 1961 their quest for delegates which culminated in his winning the 1964 Republican presidential nomination. Jockeying for the nomination in the *next* election begins the morning after for the defeated party. Shortly after the 1968 election, the 1972 prospects of Hubert Humphrey, Edward Kennedy, Edmund Muskie and others were being evaluated. When Edward Kennedy defeated Russell Long for the post of Senate Democratic Whip in 1969, the press referred to it as the beginning of his drive for the 1972 nomination.

Such endeavors take a number of forms: 1) courting of prestigious political figures whose endorsement, political skills or organization base may be helpful; 2) building national visibility and cultivating a favorable image through skillful use of mass media, personal appearances, etc.; 3) constructing alliances with state and local political organizations or building one's own *ad hoc* organizations.

The aim of such efforts is to secure the support of delegates to the national party conventions. Since the 1840s party nominations for president have been made at such conventions, and despite criticisms, are still made today in that fashion. Prior to the first national conventions, the congressional caucus was the main device. At meetings of each party's members in Congress, the presidential candidates were designated. But "King Caucus," as some of its opponents labeled it, became an unpopular device on the grounds that it was undemocratic. In the 1820s the caucus broke down and nominating was done for a while by a combination of state legislatures, public meetings and local conventions. The first national convention was convened by the Anti-Masonic party in 1831. Another group, the National Republican party held a convention to nominate Henry Clay. Also in that year the Democrats held their first convention to nominate Andrew Jackson for a second term. Thus, by 1840, national conventions had become the accepted means of nomination. See Table 1.

TABLE 1

REPUBLICAN CONVENTIONS, 1856–1968

Year	City	Date	Presidential Nominee	No. of Ballots
1856	Philadelphia	June 17–19	John C. Fremont	2
1860	Chicago	May 16–19	Abraham Lincoln	3
1864	Baltimore	June 7–8	Abraham Lincoln	1
1868	Chicago	May 20–21	Ulysses S. Grant	1
1872	Philadelphia	June 5–6	Ulysses S. Grant	1
1876	Cincinnati	June 14–16	Rutherford B. Hayes	7
1880	Chicago	June 2–8	James A. Garfield	36
1884	Chicago	June 3–6	James G. Blaine	4
1888	Chicago	June 19–25	Benjamin Harrison	8
1892	Minneapolis	June 7–10	Benjamin Harrison	1
1896	St. Louis	June 16–18	William McKinley	1
1900	Philadelphia	June 19–21	William McKinley	1
1904	Chicago	June 21–23	Theodore Roosevelt	1
1908	Chicago	June 16–19	William H. Taft	1
1912	Chicago	June 18–22	William H. Taft	1
1916	Chicago	June 7–10	Charles E. Hughes	3
1920	Chicago	June 8–12	Warren G. Harding	10
1924	Cleveland	June 10–12	Calvin Coolidge	1
1928	Kansas City	June 12–15	Herbert Hoover	1
1932	Chicago	June 14–16	Herbert Hoover	1
1936	Cleveland	June 9–12	Alfred M. Landon	1
1940	Philadelphia	June 24–28	Wendell L. Willkie	6
1944	Chicago	June 24–28	Thomas E. Dewey	1
1948	Philadelphia	June 21–25	Thomas E. Dewey	3
1952	Chicago	July 7–11	Dwight D. Eisenhower	1
1956	San Francisco	Aug. 20–23	Dwight D. Eisenhower	1
1960	Chicago	July 25–28	Richard M. Nixon	1
1964	San Francisco	July 13–16	Barry Goldwater	1
1968	Miami Beach	Aug. 5–8	Richard M. Nixon	1

TABLE 1 (*continued*)

DEMOCRATIC CONVENTIONS, 1832–1968

Year	City	Date	Presidential Nominee	No. of Ballots
1832	Baltimore	May 21	Andrew Jackson	1
1835	Baltimore	May 20	Martin Van Buren	1
1840	Baltimore	May 5	Martin Van Buren	1
1844	Baltimore	May 27–29	James K. Polk	9
1848	Baltimore	May 22–26	Lewis Cass	4
1852	Baltimore	June 1–6	Franklin Pierce	49
1856	Cincinnati	June 2–6	James Buchanan	17
1860	Baltimore	June 18–23	Stephen A. Douglas	2
1864	Chicago	August 29	George B. McClellan	1
1868	New York	July 4–11	Horatio Seymour	22
1872	Baltimore	July 9	Horace Greeley	1
1876	St. Louis	June 27–29	Samuel J. Tilden	2
1880	Cincinnati	June 22–24	Winfield S. Hancock	2
1884	Chicago	July 8–11	Grover Cleveland	2
1888	St. Louis	June 5	Grover Cleveland	1
1892	Chicago	June 21	Grover Cleveland	1
1896	Chicago	July 7	William J. Bryan	5
1900	Kansas City	July 4–6	William J. Bryan	1
1904	St. Louis	July 6–9	Alton S. Parker	1
1908	Denver	July 7–10	William J. Bryan	1
1912	Baltimore	June 25–July 2	Woodrow Wilson	46
1916	St. Louis	June 14–16	Woodrow Wilson	1
1920	San Francisco	June 28–July 6	James M. Cox	43
1924	New York	June 24–July 9	John W. Davis	103
1928	Houston	June 26–29	Alfred E. Smith	1
1932	Chicago	June 27–July 2	Franklin D. Roosevelt	4
1936	Philadelphia	June 23–27	Franklin D. Roosevelt	Acclamation
1940	Chicago	July 15–18	Franklin D. Roosevelt	1
1944	Chicago	July 19–21	Franklin D. Roosevelt	1
1948	Philadelphia	July 12–14	Harry S. Truman	1
1952	Chicago	July 21–26	Adlai E. Stevenson	3
1956	Chicago	Aug. 13–17	Adlai E. Stevenson	1
1960	Los Angeles	July 11–15	John F. Kennedy	1
1964	Atlantic City	Aug. 24–27	Lyndon B. Johnson	Acclamation
1968	Chicago	Aug. 26–29	Hubert H. Humphrey	1

SOURCE: *CQ Guide to Current American Government* (Fall 1968).

To determine the number of convention delegates for a state, each party's national committee employs a formula based partly on the state's Electoral College vote plus bonus delegates for support for the party's candidates in recent elections. The conventions are fairly large, especially the Democratic where delegates are not equated with whole votes, fractional votes being possible. In 1968, the Democrats had: 2,989 delegates and 110 national committee members casting 2,622 votes. In addition, the Democrats had 2,512 alternates. The Republicans by contrast had only 1,333 delegates and a similar number of alternates.

The apportionment formula for the 1968 Democratic convention was as follows:

1. 3 votes for each of the Electors from that state in the Electoral College.
2. a bonus of one convention vote for each 100,000 popular votes, or major fraction thereof, which were cast in the state in 1964 for presidential electors pledged to the national Democratic nominees.
3. a victory bonus of 10 votes for each state which cast its electoral votes for the 1964 Democratic nominees.
4. one vote each for the Democratic national committeeman and committeewoman from the state, said vote to be personal and incapable of exercise by any alternate.

In addition, 5 convention votes, each alloted to the Canal Zone, Guam and the Virgin Islands, and 8 to Puerto Rico (including national committeemen and committeewomen).

The result of the new voting apportionment was to further erode the proportionate strength of the South, and especially the Deep South, in the convention. In 1960, for instance, Deep South states (Alabama, Mississippi, Louisiana, Georgia, South Carolina) cast 8.7 percent of the convention vote; in 1964, 8.6 percent; and in 1968, 6.2 percent.

This formula resulted in the following distribution of votes:

TABLE 2

States	Convention Votes	States	Convention Votes
Alabama	32	New Hampshire	26
Alaska	22	New Jersey	82
Arizona	19	New Mexico	26
Arkansas	33	New York	190
California	174	North Carolina	59
Colorado	35	North Dakota	25
Connecticut	44	Ohio	115
Delaware	22	Oklahoma	41
Florida	63	Oregon	35
Georgia	43	Pennsylvania	130
Hawaii	26	Rhode Island	27
Idaho	25	South Carolina	28
Illinois	118	South Dakota	26
Indiana	63	Tennessee	51
Iowa	46	Texas	104
Kansas	38	Utah	26
Kentucky	46	Vermont	22
Louisiana	36	Virginia	54
Maine	27	Washington	47
Maryland	49	West Virginia	38
Massachusetts	72	Wisconsin	59
Michigan	96	Wyoming	22
Minnesota	52	District of	
Mississippi	24	Columbia	23
Missouri	60	Canal Zone	5
Montana	26	Guam	5
Nebraska	30	Puerto Rico	8
Nevada	22	Virgin Islands	5

SOURCE: *Congressional Quarterly Weekly Reports*, Jan. 12, 1968, p. 61.

For the 1968 Republican convention in Miami Beach, the delegates were apportioned as follows:

1. 4 delegates at-large for each state.
2. 2 delegates at-large for each representative at-large.
3. 6 additional delegates at-large for each state that voted Republican for president in 1964 or elected a Republican senator or governor in 1964 or later.

4. 1 district delegate for each congressional district which cast 2,000 votes or more for the Republican presidential nominee in 1964 or the Republican House candidate in 1966.

5. 1 additional district delegate for each congressional district which cast 10,000 votes or more for the Republican presidential nominee in 1964 or for a Republican House candidate in 1966.

6. Special allotments: District of Columbia, 9; Puerto Rico, 5; Virgin Islands, 3.

This formula resulted in the following distribution of delegates:

TABLE 3

States	Delegates	States	Delegates
Alabama	26	Nevada	12
Alaska	12	New Hampshire	8
Arizona	16	New Jersey	40
Arkansas	18	New Mexico	14
California	86	New York	92
Colorado	18	North Carolina	26
Connecticut	16	North Dakota	8
Delaware	12	Ohio	58
Florida	34	Oklahoma	22
Georgia	30	Oregon	18
Hawaii	14	Pennsylvania	64
Idaho	14	Rhode Island	14
Illinois	58	South Carolina	22
Indiana	26	South Dakota	14
Iowa	24	Tennessee	28
Kansas	20	Texas	56
Kentucky	24	Utah	8
Louisiana	26	Vermont	12
Maine	14	Virginia	24
Maryland	26	Washington	24
Massachusetts	34	West Virginia	14
Michigan	48	Wisconsin	30
Minnesota	26	Wyoming	12
Mississippi	20	District of	
Missouri	24	Columbia	9
Montana	14	Puerto Rico	5
Nebraska	16	Virgin Islands	3

SOURCE: *Congressional Quarterly Weekly Reports*, June 7, 1968, p. 1312.

There are two main ways by which national convention delegates are chosen: by assorted internal party processes—mainly combinations of state and congressional district party conventions—and by presidential primaries. But there are innumerable and bewildering variations and combinations of these devices from state to state.

Despite the publicity and furor generated by presidential primaries, the majority of states still choose their delegates through internal party processes. *Congressional Quarterly* compiled the different types of processes used to select such delegates:[17]

1. State convention selects all delegates.
2. Some delegates selected at-large by state conventions; other delegates selected at district conventions held separately from state convention (e.g., Colorado).
3. Some delegates selected at-large by entire state convention; others selected by district conventions held in conjunction with the state convention (e.g., Connecticut).
4. Delegates selected by state party committee (e.g., Arkansas).
5. Some delegates selected by state committee; others selected by district committees (e.g., Arizona).

Presidential primaries are the better known and most publicized of the two methods.[18] The primary originated in Wisconsin in 1903 where Senator Robert La Follette endorsed it as a device to weaken the power of what he called the "bosses." In 1968, one form or another was utilized in sixteen states and the District of Columbia.[19]

It is difficult to speak of a presidential primary, because there are so many variations in detail and so many possibilities for combining different elements:

1. Delegate selection only—no presidential contenders are on ballot and delegates are unpledged (e.g., New York).[20]
2. Presidential preference only—voters are confronted by the names of at least one or more of the presidential contenders and voters indicate preference. Delegates are then selected by internal party processes. Such delegates are generally required for at least one ballot to support winner of the preference poll (e.g., Indiana).

3. Two elements separated—in a number of states there is a separate poll for presidential preference and another ballot for selecting at least some convention delegates.[21] In some states the results of the preference poll are binding on delegates (e.g., Massachusetts, Oregon). But in others the results are not binding (e.g., New Jersey, New Hampshire).

4. Two elements combined—in a number of states, the presidential preference and delegate selection are combined by the device of a full slate of delegates running under the candidate's name (e.g., California) or the candidate preference appears after the name of each potential delegate (e.g., Ohio).[22]

These categories suggest the great variety; they do not, however, encompass all the possible variations. As we have mentioned even where delegates are elected, this method may apply only to part of the delegation; some may still be selected by internal party processes. The commitment of "pledged" delegates varies considerably. Some are bound by state law, but others are bound only by their personal code of honor. The states also vary over the question of whether the consent of an individual is required before his name is placed on the ballot as a candidate. In some states (e.g., Oregon, Nebraska, Wisconsin), a public official or body decides on the names to be placed on the ballot. To remove his name, the candidate must file an affidavit of non-candidacy.

State and local party leaders generally prefer to depoliticize the selection of delegates. They would generally prefer to rely on internal party processes rather than a primary. Although even these processes can become part of a vigorous internal struggle, such as the heated clash between Humphrey and McCarthy supporters for representation in the Minnesota delegation to the 1968 Democratic convention, generally a few party leaders can control the selections. If a primary is used, the leaders would prefer that it be unrelated to the selection of delegates (purely advisory) or that national figures stay out and a "favorite son" —the state governor or senator—head an uncontested unity delegation. There are a number of reasons for this preference: leaders are fearful that divisive clashes (such as Rockefeller–Goldwater in 1964, or Humphrey–Mc-Carthy–Kennedy in 1968) will create long-lasting bitterness and lead to a disunited party. In addition, they feel their own bargaining power or ability to maneuver will be greatly curtailed. Finally, they fear that they will be excluded from the state delegation because of their unwillingness to take a stand for or support a losing candidate.

Just as the methods by which delegates are selected vary, so do the approaches of candidates to those delegates.[23] One is what might be called the inside approach—attempting to win the support of state and local party leaders. Many of these will be delegates themselves or will select the delegates. Although a candidate using this approach may enter selected primaries, he does not place major stress on them. Examples would include Hubert Humphrey in 1968, Barry Goldwater in 1964 and Richard Nixon in 1960 and, to an extent, also in 1968.

A second is the public approach—attempting particularly through primary victories to demonstrate great popular support. The candidate attempts to impress the party leaders that he is their main hope of victory and that they reject him at their peril. Senator Estes Kefauver, thoroughly disliked by many party leaders, used this approach in 1952 although unsuccessfully. Both Eugene McCarthy and Robert Kennedy, until his assassination, utilized this approach in 1968.

These two approaches, however, are not mutually exclusive. Even a candidate who mainly pursues the public approach will work to cultivate party leaders behind the scenes. In 1960, while John F. Kennedy entered numerous primaries, he also placed heavy stress on private bargaining and negotiations with state and local party leaders. But party leaders will be more receptive to such efforts if the candidate can also demonstrate popularity with voters. Here the candidate may rely on past electoral performance, victories in key presidential primaries and public opinion polls. In 1964, Barry Goldwater felt compelled to enter several primaries, despite his assiduous cultivation of party activists. Indeed had he lost in the key California primary, his nomination might have been in doubt. Although Nelson Rockefeller eschewed primaries in 1968, he relied heavily on opinion polls as the basis of his contention that he could win and Nixon could not. Unfortunately for his cause, the polls were never that clearcut or his lead that overwhelming.

Participation in primaries must be seen in the context of an overall strategy to determine the outcome of the nomination struggle. Primaries may be useful tools. For example, in 1960, John Kennedy used his victory in the West Virginia primary, a predominantly Protestant state to help allay fears among many professional politicians that a Catholic could not be elected president. But rarely, if ever, have primaries alone offered access to the nomination. Rather they are one of a number of bases of influence and power.

Such intensive, pre-convention campaigns, at least in the past, made sense for only certain types of candidates. A candidate, particularly one well-endowed with financial resources, might attempt to establish himself as a front-runner with such a commanding lead, or give the appearance of one, so that no one would be able to stop him (Kennedy, 1960). A candidate without great intraparty backing might seek popular backing to compel the party to take note of his candidacy (Kefauver, 1952). Or if there is a major factional split in the party, the preliminary infighting may be important in determining the final outcome (the Eisenhower–Taft contest of 1952). On the other hand, an incumbent president (Eisenhower, 1956; Johnson, 1964) or an heir-apparent (Nixon, 1960) might engage in little overt campaigning. A potential compromise candidate, acceptable to all major elements of the party, might sit on the sidelines hopefully watching the front-runners cut each other up or lose their momentum and then have the nomination conferred on him at the convention (probably the strategy of Senator Stuart Symington of Missouri at the 1960 Democratic convention). But increasingly nominations are made on the first ballot and the pre-convention phase is decisive. Since the convention may simply ratify a decision already made, candidates cannot really afford to wait.[24]

THE CONVENTION

H. L. Mencken once declared that there is something about a national convention that makes it as fascinating as a hanging or a revival. "It is vulgar, it is ugly, it is stupid, it is tedious." [25] Yet, despite this he found it rewarding because "suddenly there comes a show so gaudy and hilarious, so melodramatic and obscene, so unimaginably exhilarating and preposterious that one lives a gorgeous year in an hour." [26]

Certainly there is a carnival aspect to a national convention. But as Frank Sorauf points out a convention in many ways is two conventions—"one of them the surface patina of bogus fun, hoopla, earnest platitudes and devotion to party symbols; the other the less public world of bargaining, influence and negotiation through which agreement is achieved and choices made." [27]

The convention, despite its critics, has a number of functions. We have already discussed its role in selecting a presidential candidate. Another function is approving a party platform. Work on this document begins even before the convention opens as a platform committee holds hearings and prepares a draft for convention approval. But a major, if not dominant role, in drafting is taken by an incumbent president, or if there is no incumbent, major contenders for a nomination will attempt to have their supporters control the product. Basically, this is a campaign document.[28] Seeking support from a variety of groups and interests, platforms are frequently ambiguous. Since both parties seek support from many of the same groups they may also tend to obscure rather than clarify the differences between the parties.

However, platforms are not without meaning. Indeed, at times, they generate major convention fights. In 1948, a floor revolt at the Democratic convention led by Hubert Humphrey, then mayor of Minneapolis, led to a strengthening of the civil-rights plank which in turn led to a withdrawal of some southern delegates. In 1964, a number of Republican governors (notably, Nelson Rockefeller, George Romney and William Scranton) waged an unsuccessful fight against the platform of the Goldwater forces. The 1968 Democratic convention saw a major fight over the plank on the Vietnam War.

The degree of ambiguity depends, as Gerald Pomper points out, on party strategy.[29] When the party seeks to appeal to a wide range of interests, ambiguity results. But when the party feels its chances would be improved by an uncompromising appeal to one group, statements become clearer. Despite many similarities between the parties, in most elections, they have disagreed on some major issues. Their disagreement was explicit in their platforms.[30] Thus, in recent years, they have disagreed over labor–management relations, farm support programs, medical care programs, defense policy, etc.

Another item on the convention agenda is the choice of a party nominee for vice-president. Rather than being chosen in an open contest on the convention floor, the decision is made by the presidential nominee closeted with party leaders and advisers; then it is ratified by the convention. An exception occurred in 1956 when the Democratic nominee Adlai Stevenson declined to state a preference and the convention after a hectic session chose Estes Kefauver over John Kennedy. But far more common was the method utilized in 1968 when Hubert Humphrey personally selected Senator Edmund Muskie of Maine and the Republican nominee Richard Nixon selected Governor Spiro Agnew of Maryland, and the respective conventions ratified the choices.[31] In selecting such a candidate, the main criterion appears to be to choose one who can bring support from important groups whether sectional, economic or religious. Although it was true in earlier nominations, recent presidential candidates now seem disinclined to name an ideological opponent to the second spot. The most recent example was probably the 1944 Republican ticket of Thomas Dewey, an internationalist and political moderate, and John W. Bricker of Ohio, an isolationist and conservative.

The chief criticism of vice-presidential nominations in the past was not so much the method as the quality of the men selected. Greater stress was placed on the balancing of the ticket than on the man's ability to be president, should the need arise. However, the recent increase in the power and prestige of the position has made men more willing to accept the nomination. Not many politicians now share one-time Vice-President John Nance Garner's assessment of the office as not even "worth a pitcher of warm spit." [32]

The convention also serves as a campaign rally on behalf of the party and its candidates before a national audience via the mass media. Orators extol the virtues of their own party while denouncing the shortcomings of the other. Such rhetoric is designed to strengthen the loyalty and renew the enthusiasm of the party faithful and attract the support of others as well. Indeed, convention officials have made some changes to strengthen its appeal to national TV audiences, such as scheduling major events during the prime evening TV viewing hours.

Like other political institutions, the convention has been criticized, and innumerable suggestions have been made for change. One proposal suggests entirely replacing the national convention with a nationwide presidential primary. Another proposal would retain the convention but extend the election of delegates to all the states. Finally, some would retain the mixed nominating system that exists—a combination of presidential primaries and internal party processes—and concentrate on internal improvements in the convention, largely procedural reforms.

As an aftermath to the 1968 Democratic convention, a committee was appointed, chaired by Senator George McGovern of South Dakota, to correct some of the alleged abuses uncovered during the pre-convention struggle. [33]

The committee came up with a rather mixed bag of rules and recommendations, to be followed by the state parties in order to qualify delegates for the 1972 convention without

challenge. Among the mandatory rulings were: full participation of 18-year-olds at every level of party activity, a requirement that minority groups, women and people under
thirty be represented on the delegation in "reasonable relationship" to the proportion of those groups in the population,
a reiteration of the decision at the Chicago convention barring the use of the unit rule (all the delegation votes are cast
for the candidate preference of the majority of delegates) and
a rule that the delegate selection process start in the calendar
year of the convention. This so-called "timeliness" requirement arose out of the controversy over the long period of time
—up to four years before the convention—during which delegates were selected. For the 1968 convention, according to the
committee as many as 1,000 delegates out of 2,622 were chosen
before the 1968 calendar year. (Former Vice-President Hubert
Humphrey received the bulk of these votes.) The committee
also prohibited practices such as proxy voting, closed slate-
making sessions and secret caucuses. It also insisted that state
parties have easily accessible rules. For example, in 1968,
twenty states either had no rules or rules so vague as to be
practically useless. Another rule bans compulsory fees for
delegates in excess of $10.00, which some state parties levy.
(The Indiana Democratic party in 1968 charged delegates
$500.)

The committee also devised rules to cover the allocation of
delegates within a state. At least 75 percent of a state delegation must come from units no larger than a congressional
district. In addition, in dividing up such delegates, a formula
must be used based equally on total population and the vote
for president in the previous national election. This was an
attempt to bolster delegates alloted to inner-city areas of the
North where heavy Democratic votes are cast. The committee,
however, reached no final decision on another issue, proportional representation. Some argued that both convention and
primary states should divide delegates on the basis of presidential preferences, rather than, as in many cases, giving the
entire delegation to the majority preference. Veterans of the

campaign of Senator Eugene McCarthy strongly supported this proposal. In state after state, they put together a substantial minority, but did not receive any delegates. The committee recommended their suggestions to the 1972 convention for a final decision. Even so, many of the rules enacted are controversial, and some states will attempt to circumvent them. Thus, unless party leaders abandon these rules, numerous challenges will probably take place at the 1972 convention.

Proposals for a national presidential primary or individual state primaries are received with some hostility by party leaders. As we pointed out earlier, they want to control the selection of delegates, thus they prefer to depoliticize the selection process. One reason is that delegates prefer to avoid open conflict which may create disunity in the party. But they also may have their own goals to pursue at the convention, such as having some bargaining power to exercise in the selection of candidates, determining the platform or placing the candidate in debt to them for future rewards (e.g., patronage).

Apart from the party organization, some broader questions about the desirability of these reforms can be raised. There is first the problem of the tremendous burden it would place on candidates in both time and resources, such as money. Second, many people would not vote in presidential primaries so the sentiments expressed would be an imperfect representation of the public. There is no convincing proof that a national presidential primary would select better candidates; for example, it is doubtful that either Wendell Willkie or Adlai Stevenson, two highly acclaimed nominees (both losers) would have entered primaries. A primary might also nominate candidates with great appeal to party regulars, but without broad appeal to the whole electorate. Thus, the present mixed system may well be better than the portrait presented by its critics. While this is not intended as a brief against reform, it is an argument for careful examination of any reform proposal in terms of its consequences for the political system. One must also be aware that for most reforms the full consequences cannot be seen until after it has been in effect for a while.

Nor do most reforms turn out to be the panacea that their proponents predicted.

☆

THE CAMPAIGN

A presidential campaign is elaborate, hectic, expensive and, at times, exciting. It imposes tremendous demands on the candidates and their supporters. The question naturally arises: what effect does the campaign have on the eventual outcome? The findings of some of the voting studies suggest three possible effects: reinforcement, activation, conversion.

One effect is that the campaign may simply reinforce or buttress existing predispositions and biases of the supporters of a particular party. The second possible effect is that the campaign may stimulate a supporter of a particular candidate to some types of overt activity; at the minimum, voting, but perhaps more—giving money, contacting other voters, etc. Finally some voters may be converted—change their preferences from one candidate to another or at least change from indecision to support for the candidate. In most elections, the number of converts is fairly small. But in a close contest, such converts may make the difference between victory and defeat.

Campaigns may have one of a number of orientations, although seldom in an absolutely pure form. Some campaigns are largely candidate oriented, stressing, in particular, the personal qualities such as vigor, decisiveness, experience, integrity, etc. Party and issues are deemphasized. The hope is that voters will be so attracted to the candidate as an individual that they will disregard traditional party loyalties and stand on issues. This may be a particularly effective strategy for a minority party to follow. But it takes a certain type of candidate, an Eisenhower, Kennedy, Lindsay, etc.

Another orientation is that of party. Stressing his label, a candidate's appeal may almost solely be based on party affiliation. If his party is dominant, traditional party loyalties hold, and his partisanship can be reinforced and activated; such an approach may be sufficient for victory.

Finally, a third approach is an issue-oriented campaign. Such issues are not very specific or detailed ones; rather they are very general, often emotion-laden ones, such as law and order, graft and corruption, fight communism, etc. All these are great simplifications of complex issues reduced to catchy phrases. Good examples of this type are Kennedy's 1960 promise to "get America moving" or Eisenhower's 1952 slogan "I shall go to Korea." Given the relatively low level of voter information and interest, an issue-oriented campaign is likely to be of this nature.

Important campaign decisions are to an extent determined by whether the candidate is the incumbent, a challenger trying to defeat the incumbent or a candidate trying to succeed a retiring incumbent of his own party. An incumbent can attempt to cloak himself in the awe and majesty of the office. He is also probably better known than his opponent and can use his experience in office as a political asset. He is in a unique position to secure vast publicity at no cost for almost anything he does and may take official action that may have political payoffs.

At the same time, there are also a number of points in the challenger's favor. Inevitably, an incumbent has done things which dissatisfy some. He has established a record which can be attacked for its omissions or commissions. The "ins" are generally blamed if something goes wrong, such as a depression; and the "outs" may receive the protest vote without much effort; even when they are without an alternative. Unburdened by official responsibilities, a challenger can engage in more free-swinging attacks.

Probably the most difficult position is that of a candidate trying to succeed a president from his own party (Stevenson, 1952; Nixon, 1960; Humphrey, 1968). It is difficult for him to extricate himself from the record of the president which may be an electoral albatross around his neck. And when he tries, he may alienate some of his own partisans while strengthening the opposition of those who were disinclined to support him. He finds himself on the defensive, in the shadow of another man, justifying a record he may have had little to do with and without adequate opportunities to present his own ideas and establish his own identity.

During a campaign, candidates are seeking a number of kinds of support: financial, party, organized groups and general electoral. With expenditures in excess of thirty million dollars for the 1968 presidential campaign, this is obviously a matter of some urgency. Fund-raising appeals run the gamut from private sessions between the candidate and large contributors, giant dinners for hundreds (frequently of dubious gastronomical value) to mass mailings and TV appeals for funds. Frequently the campaign may end with a deficit, particularly for the losing party. The candidate must also be concerned with the activation of the party regulars after the convention. He must try to heal any wounds and inspire them for the rather dreary tasks ahead—ringing doorbells, addressing envelopes, giving money, etc.

He will also be concerned with securing endorsement by organized groups. Normally each party can count on the support of some of its traditional allies, such as the Democrats relying on the AFL-CIO. But other groups may be less securely attached to the coalition and may have to be assiduously courted. The expectation, although it is not always realized, is that the followers or members of the organization will follow their leaders' advice.

Finally, candidates appeal to the general public for electoral support. But as we have already seen many voters do not have an open mind but react in terms of traditional party loyalties. Thus, a candidate and his organization must strive to get his own supporters to the polls. Next, he attempts to reach those who are independent. Finally, although there are always some converts (among weak partisans of the other camp), these are the most difficult to secure and require the greatest effort.

Presidential campaigning is a curious blend of the old

traditional time-honored methods and modern methods made possible by technology and mass communications. One time-honored method is personal contact between the candidate and the voter. Warren Harding in 1920 was probably the last stay-at-home candidate. In 1948, the then President Harry S. Truman took off in his special campaign train for his famous whistle-stop tour of the country.[34] In 1960, the Republican candidate, Richard Nixon visited all fifty states at least once in his campaign. His Democratic opponent, John Kennedy added an interesting twist as he skipped from one suburban shopping center to another via helicopter. Although presidential candidates could reach a larger audience more easily (and more safely) via television, such opportunities to see the candidate in person and to "press the flesh" are a part of the ritual of politics. No candidate is willing to dispense wholly with them. In addition, state and local candidates often feel such personal appearances may boost their prospects and insist on such visits. But their greatest impact may be in terms of activation and reinforcement since such appearances generally attract their own partisans.

Another tactic is grass roots organization to identify and mobilize one's supporters. Many hours must be spent by volunteers canvassing voters on a precinct-by-precinct basis to get them registered and then out to vote. In some cases, their efforts are borne by the party organization in that area. But if it is weak, nonexistent or hostile, the candidate may have to create an *ad hoc* personal campaign organization. To attract new people or political independents, a whole array of citizen organizations independent of the party apparatus may be established.

Television has played an increasingly large role in recent presidential elections. One of the more interesting uses, although it has not been repeated since, was the series of televised debates between Richard Nixon and John Kennedy in the months prior to the 1960 presidential election.[35] Candidates have tended of late to eschew long formal speeches on television in favor of short, spot announcements, much like the commercials for mouth washes or deodorants. The increased prominence of television as a campaign tool has led to the inclusion in the candidates' war councils of men skilled in its uses—practitioners of public relations who know how to skillfully package candidates and issues.[36] The age of television is also a costly one. In 1964 both parties spent eleven million dollars for radio and television time out of a total expenditure of twenty-nine million dollars for the presidential race.

No modern campaign is complete without its polls. These may enable a candidate to tailor his campaign to the moods and concerns of the voters. Also they may suggest where he should concentrate his efforts both in terms of geographical areas and groups of voters.

American presidential campaigns are not only complex, they are also long in duration. For years, the campaigns by tradition commenced around Labor Day and ran until the first Tuesday in November. This gave the candidates and their advisers time, following the conventions, to plan tactics and strategies for the weeks ahead. But in a very real sense, the campaign actually begins weeks before at the conventions which in many ways are giant campaign rallies. In addition, events or actions long before the conventions, such as an accelerating economic decline or an escalating war, may have more impact on the eventual outcome than the campaign itself. An incumbent, who is a skilled practitioner of politics, will attempt to use the power and resources of his office to structure the campaign in ways favorable to him. And his potential challengers, far in advance of the campaign, look for his mistakes and weaknesses and attempt to adopt causes and project an image that will command public recognition and approval.

Because of the length of the campaign and the numerous distractions for the electorate, it is a real test of the ingenuity of the candidates and their supporters to secure and keep the attention of the electorate. It is as well a time of tremendous uncertainties and inevitable insecurities which even modern scientific measuring devices cannot entirely alleviate.

☆

THE ELECTION

There are a number of ways to classify presidential elections. One way is in their relation to the pattern of party identification within the electorate. Angus Campbell and his associates at the Survey Research Center of the University of Michigan devised the following typology:[37]

1. Maintaining election:

These reflect the existing pattern of party identification within the electorate. The majority party is retained in power (e.g., 1900, 1904, 1908, 1924, 1928, 1936, 1940, 1944, 1948).

2. Deviating election:

In such an election, as a result of an issue or issues or a particular candidate (or some combination thereof) the normal majority loses the White House. But while this party is displaced from power, it is only a temporary aberration, the basic pattern of party loyalty is not altered. For example, 1952 and 1956 are regarded as deviating elections. While a Republican presidential candidate (Eisenhower) prevailed, the pattern of party identification remained strongly Democratic. Indeed, during six of his eight years in the White House, Eisenhower faced a Congress controlled by the opposition party.

3. Reinstating election:

Such an election occurs when the dominant party (in terms of party identification) is returned to power after a deviating election or two. In 1960 the Democrats recaptured the presidency after the two electoral victories of Eisenhower. The normal majority reasserted itself.[38] Another example would be 1920 when the Republicans, the dominant party since the Civil War, recaptured the White House after Wilson's two victories.

4. Realigning election:

Here a marked and long-run shift occurs in the division of party identification in the country. The minority becomes the new "normal" majority. The election of 1932 would be an example. In this case, the New Deal coalition destroyed the hegemony of the Republican party which had largely endured since the Civil War. Some commentators suggest that with the election of 1968 we are moving into a period of considerable political upheaval and the beginning of a realignment.[39] As evidence, they cite a number of facts: in the past, realignments in voting behavior have always been signaled by the rise of significant third parties. The American Independent party of George Wallace in 1968 showed considerable strength and some degree of persistence beyond the presidential election. There is also the recent fluidity of American politics: an impressive growth in the number of political independents and a liquidation of pre-existing party commitments by individual voters. However, unlike the past when in such realignments a new dominant party developed, Walter Burnham suggests that what is developing is a politics without parties rather than a recrystallization and revitalization of political parties.[40]

Another way of classifying presidential elections is according to the nature of the decision rendered. Some elections, what V. O. Key called "critical elections" seem to mark turning points in electoral politics. They seem to decide clusters of issues in a fairly clear-cut way more so than most elections.[41] There is also considerable agreement among historians with regard to these elections. The first came in 1800 when Thomas Jefferson destroyed the Federalist hegemony established in the early days of the republic by Washington, Hamilton and Adams. Another came in 1828 with the election of Andrew Jackson. A third was the election in 1860 of Abraham Lincoln that was shortly followed by the Civil War. In 1896, another occurred with the election of William McKinley and brought the domination of industrial capitalism. This system endured until its collapse in the Depression of the 1930s, the victory of Franklin D. Roosevelt in 1932 and the establishment of various welfare policies.

The results of the presidential election not only decide who is going to occupy the White House for the next four years, but have an impact on other electoral races as well. Every four years congressional elections occur at the same time as the presidential election, and such decisions are closely linked. In a recent study, it was reported that over a forty-four year period, in only 18 percent of the House districts did a majority of voters support a presidential candidate of one party while voting for the opposition party's candidate for the House.[42] Similarly, senatorial elections are also closely tied in with the results of the presidential contest. As the margin of the victorious presidential candidate in the state increases, the chance of his party holding or gaining the Senate seat increases. However, senators find it less difficult to establish their own political visibility and independent identity than do representatives; thus, they can more easily survive a trend against their party.[43] Also in a study of split-ticket voting, Campbell and Miller reported that the most common pattern was to vote a straight ticket for national candidates (president, senators, representatives) and to split at state and local levels.[44]

Voters generally have a better developed image of presidential than congressional candidates. As a result, a presidential candidate may attract voters not only to himself, but to other candidates on the ticket, the so-called "coattail" theory. Actually a presidential candidate's drawing power is not even throughout the country. In areas where his party is traditionally strong (e.g., Democrats in the South), its congressional candidates generally run ahead of the presidential candidate. But in areas where the party is weaker (e.g., a Republican presidential candidate in the South), the presidential candidate will generally run ahead of the congressional candidates. It is in marginal areas, where the parties are fairly evenly matched, that the coattails of the presidential candidate seem to have the greatest drawing power. Thus, in the less competitive areas, the dominant party will generally hold onto its congressional seats, although perhaps by somewhat reduced margins. But, in marginal areas, the additional voters drawn to the ticket by the presidential candidate may provide the margin needed for congressional victory as well.[45]

In off-year elections (e.g., 1970) when the presidency is not at stake, there are also certain general patterns. Mid-term elections are generally a source of trouble for the party holding the presidency for, almost without exception, it loses seats.[46] Off-year elections following extremely close presidential elections such as 1960 and 1968 may deviate from the pattern. In 1962, two years after Kennedy's narrow victory over Nixon, the Democrats lost House seats, but gained Senate seats. Similarly in 1970, the Republicans lost seats in the House, but gained in the Senate. An off-year election is frequently viewed as a sort of referendum on the record of the administration. Most recent presidents in taking to the campaign trail in off-year elections seem to view it this way, at least in part. In 1970, President Nixon, as well as Vice-President Agnew campaigned vigorously for Republican congressional candidates. Voter reaction, however, is almost uniformly negative, although greater in some years than others.

There are other factors at work besides possible voter dissatisfaction with the administration. Voter participation drops considerably in off-year elections as compared to a presidential election. For example, in 1966, 48 percent of those eligible voted compared with 61.6 percent in 1968. The greatest dropout comes from the less interested and committed. With the absence of the drama and excitement found in the presidential race, they are not stimulated to vote. Thus the decline in the support for the president's party may result more from the absence of its earlier supporters at the polls than from a reaction against the administration. And such congressional losses generally occur in marginal districts and states where a loss of a few votes can reverse the results.

The absence of the centralizing influence of the presidential race may also permit greater emphasis on local problems, personalities and issues. This factor complicates the off-year election and makes it difficult to discern what the results actually mean.

☆
THE ELECTORAL COLLEGE[47]

This singular American institution adds an additional note of complexity to presidential elections. It gives a special form to electoral competition, affects the tactics of the candidates and may affect the outcome in its own peculiar way.

The Electoral College emerged at the Constitutional Convention as a compromise among the diverse schemes for selecting the chief executive. Among the proposed methods was selection by the legislature and election by direct vote of the people. Election by intermediate electors blended features of both plans.

The Electoral College system provides a double election. Instead of voting directly for president, voters legally vote for a slate of presidential electors equal to the number of senators and representatives from their state.

The total membership of the college is 538—the sum of the membership of the Senate (100), the House (435) and the three votes of the District of Columbia, by provision of the 23rd amendment to the Constitution.

After the election the winning slate of electors in each state (the slate pledged to the presidential candidate who received the most votes in the state) convene in their respective state capitols in early December to cast their votes. Thus in a sense, it is a series of electoral colleges, not a single electoral college. In early January the votes are counted before a joint session of Congress.[48] The Constitution provides that the president and vice-president be elected by an absolute majority (270 votes). If such a majority does not exist (as is likely with three or more candidates), the Constitution sets up what is, in effect, a "super-electoral college." The election for president is thrown into the House of Representatives where the members may choose among the three highest candidates. However, each state delegation has only one vote, rather than each member voting individually. The election of vice-president is thrown into the Senate, with each member having one vote.

TABLE 4

State	Electoral Vote	State	Electoral Vote
Alabama	10	Missouri	12
Alaska	3	Montana	4
Arizona	5	Nebraska	5
Arkansas	6	Nevada	3
California	40	New Hampshire	4
Colorado	6	New Jersey	17
Connecticut	8	New Mexico	4
Delaware	3	New York	43
District of		North Carolina	13
Columbia	3	North Dakota	4
Florida	14	Ohio	26
Georgia	12	Oklahoma	8
Hawaii	4	Oregon	6
Idaho	4	Pennsylvania	29
Illinois	26	Rhode Island	4
Indiana	13	South Carolina	8
Iowa	9	South Dakota	4
Kansas	7	Tennessee	11
Kentucky	9	Texas	25
Louisiana	10	Utah	4
Maine	4	Vermont	3
Maryland	10	Virginia	12
Massachusetts	14	Washington	9
Michigan	21	West Virginia	7
Minnesota	10	Wisconsin	12
Mississippi	7	Wyoming	3

SOURCE: *Congressional Quarterly Almanac* (1966), p. 946. Reprinted by permission.

The states are authorized by the Constitution to appoint their electors "in such manner as the legislature thereof directs." In the first few elections, the electors were selected chiefly by the state legislatures. But with the development of a party system, the choice was put in the hands of the public as it chose among electors put forth by the parties. At first, a district system was utilized, each district having one elector. Such districts frequently coincided with congressional districts. But by 1836, the district system was abandoned, replaced by a state-wide ticket of electors. Whereas the district system frequently produced a divided vote from a state, the state-wide system was based on "winner take all." The candidate, who carries the state with the most votes no matter how small the plurality, gets all the electoral vote.

TABLE 5

VOTE FOR PRESIDENT SINCE 1900

Year	Candidates	Popular Vote Total	Per- centage	Electoral Vote Received
1900	William McKinley (R)	7,219,828	51.7	271
	William J. Bryan (D)	6,358,160	45.5	155
	Others	396,200	2.8	—
1904	Theodore Roosevelt (R)	7,628,831	56.4	336
	Alton B. Parker (D)	5,084,533	37.6	140
	Eugene V. Debs (S)	402,714	3.0	—
	Silas C. Swallow (P)	259,163	1.9	—
	Others	149,357	1.1	—
1908	William H. Taft (R)	7,679,114	51.6	321
	William J. Bryan (D)	6,410,665	43.1	162
	Eugene V. Debs (S)	420,858	2.8	—
	Eugene W. Chafin (P)	252,704	1.7	—
	Others	127,379	.9	—
1912	Woodrow Wilson (D)	6,301,254	41.9	435
	Theodore Roosevelt (PR)	4,127,788	27.4	88
	William H. Taft (R)	3,485,831	23.2	8
	Eugene V. Debs (S)	901,255	6.0	—
	Others	238,934	1.6	—
1916	Woodrow Wilson (D)	9,131,511	49.3	277
	Charles E. Hughes (R)	8,548,935	46.1	254
	Allan L. Benson (S)	585,974	3.2	—
	Others	269,812	1.5	—
1920	Warren G. Harding (R)	16,153,115	60.3	404
	James M. Cox (D)	9,133,092	34.1	127
	Eugene V. Debs (S)	915,490	3.4	—
	Others	566,916	2.1	—

TABLE 5 (*continued*)

Year	Candidates	Popular Vote Total	Per-centage	Electoral Vote Received
1924	Calvin Coolidge (R)	15,719,921	54.9	382
	John W. Davis (D)	8,386,704	28.8	136
	Robert M. LaFollette (PR)	4,832,532	16.6	13
	Others	155,866	.5	—
1928	Herbert C. Hoover (R)	21,437,277	58.2	444
	Alfred E. Smith (D)	15,007,698	40.8	87
	Others	360,976	1.0	—
1932	Franklin D. Roosevelt (D)	22,829,501	57.4	472
	Herbert C. Hoover (R)	15,760,684	39.6	59
	Norman M. Thomas (S)	884,649	2.2	—
	Others	283,925	.8	—
1936	Franklin D. Roosevelt (D)	27,313,041	60.8	523
	Alfred M. Landon (R)	16,684,231	36.5	8
	William Lemke (U)	892,267	2.0	—
	Others	320,932	.7	—
1940	Franklin D. Roosevelt (D)	27,313,041	54.7	449
	Wendell Willkie (R)	22,348,480	44.8	82
	Others	238,897	.5	—
1944	Franklin D. Roosevelt (D)	25,612,610	53.4	432
	Thomas E. Dewey R	22,017,617	45.9	99
	Others	346,443	.7	—
1948	Harry S. Truman (D)	24,179,345	49.6	303
	Thomas E. Dewey (R)	21,991,291	45.1	189
	J. Strom Thurmond (SRD)	1,176,125	2.4	39
	Henry A. Wallace (PR)	1,157,326	2.4	—
	Others	289,739	.6	—

TABLE 5 (*continued*)

Year	Candidates	Popular Vote Total	Per-centage	Electoral Vote Received
1952	Dwight D. Eisenhower (R)	33,936,234	55.1	442
	Adlai E. Stevenson (D)	27,314,992	44.4	89
	Others	299,692	.5	—
1956	Dwight D. Eisenhower (R)	35,590,472	57.4	457
	Adlai E. Stevenson (D)	26,022,752	42.0	73
	Unpledged Elector Slates[1]	196,318	.3	—
	Others	217,366	.3	1
1960[2]	John F. Kennedy (D)	34,220,984	49.5	303
	Richard M. Nixon (R)	34,108,157	49.3	219
	Unpledged Elector Slates[1]	638,822	.9	15
	Others	188,559	.3	—
1964	Lyndon B. Johnson (D)	43,129,484	61.1	486
	Barry M. Goldwater (R)	27,178,188	38.5	52
	Others	336,838	.4	—
1968	Richard M. Nixon (R)	31,785,480	43.4	301
	Hubert H. Humphrey (D)	31,275,165	42.7	191
	George Wallace (AI)	9,906,473	13.5	46
	Others	244,444	.4	—

[1] Largely from Southern states where the Democratic party was hostile to the national party nominee and offered electors that were unpledged, rather than pledged to national candidate.

[2] A different popular vote total and percentage for John F. Kennedy of 34,049,976 (49.2 percent) is based on an alternative method of determining popular vote in Alabama. Under this method the unpledged elector slates received 491,527 votes (.7 percent). For details, see Pierce, *The People's President*, pp. 102–104.

SOURCE: Figures taken from *Congressional Quarterly Guide to American Government* (Spring 1968), 55–56. Reprinted by permission. For 1968 only, from *CQ Weekly Report*, June 6, 1969, 884.

The state-by-state breakdown for the 1968 presidential election was as follows:

TABLE 6

1968 PRESIDENTIAL ELECTION RESULTS

(270 Electoral Votes Needed to Win)

State	ELECTORAL VOTE Nixon	Humphrey	Wallace	Plurality
Alabama	—	—	10	438,157 AI
Alaska	3	—	—	878 R
Arizona	5	—	—	80,212 R
Arkansas	—	—	6	48,005 AI
California	40	—	—	222,190 R
Colorado	6	—	—	72,990 R
Connecticut	—	8	—	66,989 D
Delaware	3	—	—	7,432 R
District of Columbia	—	3	—	106,835 D
Florida	14	—	—	165,878 R
Georgia	—	—	12	144,123 AI
Hawaii	—	4	—	49,916 D
Idaho	4	—	—	75,194 R
Illinois	26	—	—	128,920 R
Indiana	13	—	—	257,969 R
Iowa	9	—	—	141,902 R
Kansas	7	—	—	168,282 R
Kentucky	9	—	—	54,394 R
Louisiana	—	—	10	219,116 AI
Maine	—	4	—	48,007 D
Maryland	—	10	—	17,371 D
Massachusetts	—	14	—	695,957 D
Michigan	—	21	—	238,319 D
Minnesota	—	10	—	186,435 D
Mississippi	—	—	7	255,430 AI
Missouri	12	—	—	14,147 R
Montana	4	—	—	20,901 R
Nebraska	5	—	—	140,437 R
Nevada	3	—	—	14,932 R
New Hampshire	4	—	—	23,322 R
New Jersey	17	—	—	53,717 R
New Mexico	4	—	—	39,022 R
New York	—	43	—	373,150 D
North Carolina	13	—	—	128,825 R
North Dakota	4	—	—	40,818 R
Ohio	26	—	—	93,105 R
Oklahoma	8	—	—	148,039 R
Oregon	6	—	—	45,362 R

TABLE 6 (*continued*)

State	ELECTORAL VOTE Nixon	Humphrey	Wallace	Plurality
Pennsylvania	—	29	—	212,162 D
Rhode Island	—	4	—	123,568 D
South Carolina	8	—	—	48,804 R
South Dakota	4	—	—	29,313 R
Tennessee	11	—	—	46,188 R
Texas	—	25	—	41,417 D
Utah	4	—	—	81,565 R
Vermont	3	—	—	14,679 R
Virginia	12	—	—	142,840 R
Washington	—	9	—	41,818 D
West Virginia	—	7	—	66,781 D
Wisconsin	12	—	—	59,650 R
Wyoming	3	—	—	25,200 R
TOTAL	302	191	45	312,605 R

SOURCE: *CQ Almanac*, 24 (1968), p. 946. Reprinted with permission.

As the parties took over the task of selecting electors, the Electoral College declined as a deliberative body. Hamilton had seen the electors as those "most likely to possess the information and discernment requisite to such complicated investigations." [49] But with the development of parties, the electors were mainly a party slate, pledged to support the presidential and vice-presidential candidate of their party. In most states, they are selected by the convention or state committee of their party. In addition, many states no longer print the names of the electors on the ballot; they only list the names of the presidential and vice-presidential candidates. But, regardless of their absence the legal effect is the same; you are voting for a slate of electors.

Occasionally an elector votes in December for a candidate other than the one whose slate he is on. For example in 1968, an elector from North Carolina pledged to Nixon, voted for George Wallace. The number in any one election is usually only one or two and has not affected the outcome, but the potential for mischief is there in case of a close contest. In only a small number of states are electors legally bound to vote for their party or candidate. In most states, such a commitment rests on party loyalty or honor. There appears to be no viable legal means of enforcing such a commitment.[50]

The Electoral College has been subject to rather constant criticism and the cause of dire warnings. Critics have attacked it for some of its results, the possibilities for mischief and breakdown and its violation of democratic tenets because of its differential impact on groups and interests in the country.

First, as to its results: the Electoral College has failed in three instances to select a president (1800, 1824 and 1876). In the first two instances, the decision was made by a contingency election (selection in the House). In 1876, Congress established an electoral commission to rule on disputed sets of electoral returns from several Southern states. But in a number of other instances, the shift of a few votes in several crucial states would have deprived any candidate of the requisite majority and thrown it into the House (1916, 1948, 1960, 1968). Such an eventuality removes the decision even further from the electorate and opens the door to bargaining and intrigue within Congress.

In two instances, the candidate selected in the Electoral College had fewer popular votes than his opponent (1876, 1888).[51] This produced what has been called, "a minority president." And in a number of other elections the shift of a few votes would have produced other "minority presidents."

Some observers are concerned with the possibilities for mischief in the system. Thus, in close contests, a few electors by violating their pledge could deprive any candidate of the necessary majority in the college, throwing the election into Congress. They also point out that with three or more major presidential candidates, it is very likely that no candidate will get a majority. This might enable one of the candidates to offer his electoral votes to one of the other candidates in return for some concessions. This was believed to be George Wallace's plan in 1968. If he could have carried enough states to deprive both Humphrey and Nixon of the required number of electors, then he could have used his electors to bargain with them prior to the December meeting of the college. In return for concessions (such as lax enforcement of civil-rights policies, school integration, etc.), he would have given one of them his votes.

The provision for a contingency election in the House is also criticized, particularly its one vote per state. Thus the majority of the state delegation (probably along partisan lines) would decide how the vote would be cast, irrespective of the results in their state. It would also open the door to considerable bargaining and logrolling in Congress. The doubt and uncertainty over who is president would also continue for a number of months, possibly immobilizing the government.

But, as Frank Sorauf points out, behind the attempts to reform or abolish the Electoral College are broad questions of power and ideology. "Electoral systems like other political institutions are allocators of political power in that they create political advantages for some which they deny to others." [52] The Electoral College enhances the political power of large urbanized, industrial states like New York, California, Illinois, etc. It particularly enhances the power of well-organized religious, ethnic or economic groups that are concentrated in such pivotal states. This power is primarily based on the "winner take all" tradition, rather than the Electoral College itself. Such power, is alleged to serve as a counterbalance to the magnified political power of rural, small town areas as reflected in Congress. Thus, one's reactions to reform or the type of reform one proposes is related to how one feels about such groups and the goals or policies they espouse.

Another issue is that of direct popular democracy itself, which, according to some critics of the Electoral College, necessitates its abolition or, at least, the elimination of any real discretion in the outcome. And in many respects, the Electoral College has evolved into something close to a *de facto* popular election. Some of the reforms simply try to accelerate this development.

There are diverse proposals to "reform" the Electoral College.[53] One, proposed by President Johnson in 1967 would simply abolish the office of elector, and have the electoral vote automatically cast in accordance with the popular vote. This would prevent episodes such as that in 1968 when one Nixon elector voted for another candidate. This reform, however, still retains the "winner take all" concept.

A second plan would restore the district system that was utilized in the early days of the republic. Under this plan two electors would be chosen state-wide. The state would be divided into districts equal to the number of seats it possessed in the House (lines could be the same as House district lines). The presidential candidate who gets the most votes in the district would win the elector. It would retain the requirement of a majority of electors to win (some versions require only 40 percent) and it would give the House and Senate jointly the power to make a decision, if no candidate got the required margin in the Electoral College. This plan has generally found support in rural and less populous states since it would weaken the power of the large industrial states. One of its major defects is the possibility it opens for manipulating the district lines for partisan advantage.

Another plan would do away with the "winner take all" aspect of the present system and award the votes on a proportional basis; if a candidate gets 65 percent of the popular vote in a state, he gets the same percentage of the state electoral vote rather than all of it. The plan would also abolish the office of elector. If no candidate got 40 percent of the vote, the election would be thrown into Congress, with each member having one vote. There is some evidence, however, that this plan, if in effect in the past, would also have produced some minority presidents because of the way the popular votes were distributed (1880, 1896). In addition much of the enthusiasm expressed for this plan in the 1950s has been transferred to the next plan to be discussed.

This plan would abolish both electors and electoral votes; the president would be chosen by direct popular vote. In 1969, a proposed amendment, embodying this proposal passed the House as the proposed 26th amendment. It also provides for a runoff among the top two candidates, if no one received at least 40 percent of the popular vote. This plan, according to its defenders, has a number of attractions: it is in accord with basic democratic theory. It would eliminate the possibility of a minority president and eliminate the possibilities for manipulating electors or congressmen. On the other hand some critics argue that it would undermine the two-party system by encouraging third parties and necessitate bargaining and logrolling if a runoff election were necessary. Such a runoff election would place additional burdens on already hard-pressed candidates, their supporters and their treasuries.

One of the difficulties in reforming the Electoral College is the difficulty of securing a consensus: while many agree on the need or desirability of change, the form or type of change is another matter. In the past the greatest changes have come by custom, tradition or state laws, not by constitutional amendment.

☆

TENURE OF OFFICE

According to the Constitution, the term for which a president is elected is four years. Until the adoption of the 22nd Amendment, a president legally was eligible indefinitely for reelection. But until Franklin D. Roosevelt's victory for a third term in 1940, no other president had won more than two terms. Thus a sort of unwritten custom developed barring a third term. In the 1940 campaign Roosevelt's bid was attacked both within and outside his party as a violation of this custom. He was not only successful, but he also won an unprecedented fourth term in 1944.

During the Truman presidency the 22nd Amendment was adopted which declares that "no president shall be elected to the office of President more than twice." In the case of a vice-president who succeeded to the presidency, it provides that if he serves for more than two years of someone else's term, he may run only once in his own right.

A careful student of the presidency has labeled the amendment a "mixture of political motivation, partisan and personal." [54] In many respects it was revenge against Roosevelt for breaking the tradition against a third term. It was also an attack on a strong executive by legislators irked at their relative decline in power. But despite the motivations in adopting it, Louis Koenig sees it as instilling certain weaknesses in the office.[55] It may weaken a president's authority during his second and final term. During a crisis, it might compel a change in leadership if the president were at the end of his term. Finally, Koenig considers it as basically antidemocratic, denying the electorate the opportunity to choose a man three or more times if they so choose.

SUCCESSION TO THE PRESIDENCY OTHER THAN BY ELECTION

The Constitution makes provision for succession to the office of president if the incumbent dies, resigns or is unable to perform his duties, by establishing the office of vice-president. Eight presidents have died while in office:

TABLE 7

INCOMPLETED TERMS OF PRESIDENTS

President	Term	Succeeded by
William Henry Harrison	3/4/1841–4/4/1841	John Tyler
Zachary Taylor	3/5/1849–7/9/1850	Millard Fillmore
Abraham Lincoln	3/4/1865–4/15/1865 (second term)	Andrew Johnson
James A. Garfield	3/4/1881–9/19/1881	Chester A. Arthur
William McKinley	3/4/1901–9/14/1901 (second term)	Theodore Roosevelt
Warren G. Harding	3/4/1921–8/2/1923	Calvin Coolidge
Franklin D. Roosevelt	1/20/1945–4/12/1945 (fourth term)	Harry S. Truman
John F. Kennedy	1/20/1961–11/22/1963	Lyndon B. Johnson

SOURCE: *CQ Guide to Current American Government* (Spring 1968), 72. Reprinted by permission.

No president has resigned. Although several presidents were disabled for periods of time (Garfield, Wilson, Eisenhower), until the adoption of the 25th Amendment, there were no prescribed procedures for establishing such disability. Without such procedures, a vice-president was reluctant to move for fear he would be viewed as a usurper and his actions be the basis of a constitutional crisis. A number of recent presidents reached informal understandings with their vice-presidents on this issue (Eisenhower, Kennedy, Johnson).

Such encounters with presidential disability and the constitutional, legal and administrative problems it posed led to the adoption of the 25th Amendment in 1967. Disability may not be limited to physical illness, but also extends to mental illness or a president who is missing or captured. The determination of presidential disability can be made either by the president himself or by the vice-president acting with a majority of the cabinet or some other body provided by Congress. In such cases, the vice-president is to act as acting president. Finally, the end of presidential disability can be determined by either the president or, in the event the vice-president and cabinet or other body do not agree, the issue is to be resolved by Congress. While certainly not a perfect solution, the amendment tends to clear up some ambiguities and provide some rules and procedures for dealing with a potentially serious problem.

The 1967 amendment also dealt with another problem: a vacancy in the office of vice-president. Seven vice-presidents have died in office. One Vice-President, John C. Calhoun (March 4, 1829–December 28, 1832) resigned during the Andrew Jackson Administration to become a senator. In the past, when a vice-president succeeded to the presidency on the death of the incumbent, the vice-presidency remained vacant until the next election. But under the terms of the 25th amendment, the office can now be filled. It empowers the president to nominate a vice-president subject to congressional confirmation (majority vote in both houses).

TABLE 8

INCOMPLETED TERMS OF VICE-PRESIDENTS

Vice-President	Term	President at Time
George Clinton	3/4/1809–4/20/1812 (second term)	James Madison
Elbridge Gerry	3/4/1813–11/23/1814	James Madison
William R. King	3/4/1853–4/18/1853	Franklin Pierce
Henry Wilson	3/4/1873–11/22/1875	Ulysses S. Grant
Thomas A. Hendricks	3/4/1885–11/25/1885	Grover Cleveland
Garret A. Hobart	3/4/1897–11/21/1899	William McKinley
James S. Sherman	3/4/1909–10/30/1912	William H. Taft

SOURCE: *CQ Guide to Current American Government* (Spring 1968), 72. Reprinted by permission.

This provision may also largely eliminate the possibility of another problem, a double vacancy, the office of president and vice-president both being vacant. Formerly, this was a very real possibility as long as no provision existed to fill a vacancy in the vice-presidential office. Thus, if the vice-president succeeded to the presidency and then died, there was no clearly defined constitutional line of succession. However, by law, Congress has provided for such an eventuality by establishing a line of succession to the presidency after the vice-president. Vacillating between placing congressional leaders and cabinet members first in the line, Congress passed three laws on the subject. The latest, in 1947, placed the speaker of the house next in line after the vice-president, next came the president pro tempore of the Senate and then the cabinet members commencing with the secretary of State. Under an earlier act, the cabinet was placed next in line after the vice-president. But neither act really faced the grim possibility that in a future nuclear war the whole list of successors could be wiped out in a single blow.

In this chapter considerable attention has been devoted to the president's electoral arena. But this is easily justified. The way in which an individual secures and retains his position cannot help but affect the way he subsequently behaves. Thus for the president the electoral process is very much a part of his world shaping and focusing his outlook and conduct.

NOTES

1. Probably the best book on this topic is Nelson W. Polsby and Aaron B. Wildavsky, *Presidential Elections,* 2nd ed. (New York: Charles Scribner's Sons, 1968).

2. V. O. Key, Jr. *Politics, Parties and Pressure Groups,* 5th ed. (New York: Thomas Y. Crowell Co., 1964), p. 653.

3. See Frank Sorauf, *Party Politics in America* (Boston: Little Brown and Co., 1968), p. 256.

4. Ibid., p. 299.

5. Ibid., pp. 297–300.

6. E. E. Schattschneider, *Party Government* (New York: Rinehart, 1942), p. 129.

7. Sorauf, pp. 273–74.

8. For some interesting studies of state parties, see Leon D. Epstein, *Politics in Wisconsin* (Madison: University of Wisconsin Press, 1958), John H. Fenton, *Midwest Politics* (New York: Holt, Rinehart, and Winston, Inc., 1966), and Duane Lockard, *New England State Politics* (Princeton: Princeton University Press, 1959).

9. See an attempt to classify types of state organizations in Lockard, pp. 325–26.

10. See, for example, Angus Campbell, *et al., The American Voter* (New York: John Wiley & Son, 1960).

11. See Walter Dean Burnham, "Election 1968—The Abortive Landslide," *Transaction,* December 1968, 21.

12. See the Gallup Poll in Detroit *Free Press,* December 14, 1969, 14B.

13. See Campbell, Chapter 10 for these categories and examples of the responses to interviewers.

14. Ibid., p. 244.

15. See Gerald Pomper, *Elections in America* (New York: Dodd, Mead and Co., 1968), pp. 95–98.

16. For a more detailed study of the nominating process, see Gerald Pomper, *Nominating the President* (New York: W. W. Norton and Co., 1966). Also relevant chapters in Polsby and Wildavsky.

17. See *Congressional Quarterly Weekly Report* (May 26, 1967), 895.

18. See James W. Davis, *Presidential Primaries: Road to the White House* (New York: Thomas Y. Crowell Co., 1967).

19. For the legal details and the 1968 results, see *C.Q. Guide to American Government* (Fall 1968), 26–28 and *CQ Weekly Report* (May 26, 1967), 893–98. *CQ* uses the figure fourteen plus the ˙District of Columbia because they excluded Alabama and New York. I included them because of the way I classified presidential primaries.

20. May not apply to all delegates. In New York, only district delegates are selected by election; delegates at-large are selected by state party committee.

21. In Illinois delegates at-large are selected by state convention.

22. The classification scheme used here was found in Sorauf, pp. 263–66.

23. For some graphic accounts of pre-convention activities including primaries, see Theodore H. White, *The Making of the President 1960* (New York: Atheneum, 1961), especially Chapters 4, 5 and 7, or his subsequent accounts of 1964 and 1968.

24. See a classification of patterns of leadership selection for presidential nominations in Paul T. David, *et al.*, *The Politics of National Party Conventions* (Washington: The Brookings Institution, 1960), p. 117.

25. *H. L. Mencken on Politics,* ed. Malcolm Moos (New York: Random House, 1960), p. 83.

26. Ibid.

27. Sorauf, pp. 279–80.

28. See party platforms for past years compiled in one volume, Kirk H. Porter and Donald B. Johnson, *National Party Platforms 1840–1964* (Urbana: University of Illinois Press, 1966).

29. See Pomper, *Elections in America,* pp. 69–71.

30. Ibid., pp. 72–73 for such a listing.

31. For an account of the selection of Agnew, see Theodore H. White, *The Making of the President, 1968* (New York: Atheneum, 1969), pp. 249–53. A revolt on the floor centering around the nomination of George Romney of Michigan was easily defeated.

32. Quoted in Theodore H. White, *The Making of the President, 1960* (New York: Atheneum, 1961), pp. 175–76.

33. For some suggested reforms of this character, see Senator George McGovern, "The Lessons of 1968," *Harper's Magazine,* January 1970, 43–47; also see *The New Republic,* February 7, 1970, 9–10.

34. For a memorable account, see Irwin D. Ross, *The Loneliest Campaign: The Truman Victory of 1948* (New York: New American Library, 1968).

35. For more detail on the debates and analysis of their impact, see *The Great Debates,* ed. Sidney Kraus (Bloomington: Indiana University Press, 1962).

36. For an insider's account of the utilization of television by the Nixon camp in 1968, see Joe McGinnis, *The Selling of a President* (New York: Trident Press, 1969). See Stanley Kelley, Jr., *Professional Public Relations and Political Power* (Baltimore: Johns Hopkins University Press, 1956) for a broader treatment of the topic. Also see Dan Nimmo, *The Political Persuaders* (Englewood Cliffs, New Jersey: Prentice-Hall, 1970).

37. See Campbell, *et al.,* especially Chapter 19.

38. See Philip E. Converse, Angus Campbell, Warren E. Miller and Donald E. Stokes, "Stability and Change in 1960: A Reinstating Election," *American Political Science Review,* June 1961, 269–80.

39. See Walter Dean Burnham, "The End of American Party Politics," *Transaction,* December 1969, 12–22.

40. Ibid., pp. 20–22.

41. See V. O. Key, Jr., "A Theory of Critical Elections," *Journal of Politics,* 1955, 3–18.

42. See Milton C. Cummings, Jr., *Congressmen and the Electorate* (New York: Free Press, 1966), pp. 10–11.

43. See V. O. Key, Jr., *Politics, Parties and Pressure Groups,* 5th ed. (New York: Thomas Y. Crowell Co., 1964), pp. 548–53.

44. Angus Campbell and Warren Miller, "Motivational Basis of Straight-Ticket Voting," *American Political Science Review,* June 1957, 294.

45. See Charles Press, "Voting Statistics and Presidential Coattails," *American Political Science Review,* December 1958, 1941–50.

46. See Charles Press, "Prediction of Mid-term Elections," *Western Political Quarterly,* 1956, 691–98.

47. On the Electoral College, see more detailed treatment in Lucius Wilmerding, *The Electoral College* (New Brunswick; Rutgers University Press, 1958); also Neal Pierce, *The People's President* (New York: Simon and Schuster, 1968).

48. In 1969, Hubert Humphrey, the defeated Democratic nominee had the dubious honor as President of the Senate to proclaim the official victory of his opponent, Richard Nixon. See *Congressional Record,* 91st Congress, 1st Session (January 6, 1969), H70. Nixon had to perform the same task in 1960 proclaiming John F. Kennedy President; see *Congressional Record* 87th Congress, 1st Session (January 6, 1961), 291.

49. See Number 68 of any edition of *The Federalist,* an American political classic.

50. See congressional debate in 1969 over whether to throw out the vote of the North Carolina elector in *Congressional Record,* 91st Congress, 1st Session (January 6, 1969), H46–H70. The decision was to accept the vote as cast.

51. Some other instances are less clear-cut: (1824), see Pierce, pp. 82–86; (1960), ibid., pp. 100–109.

52. See Sorauf, p. 260.

53. For an enumeration and discussion of them as well as a history of such efforts, see Pierce, Chapters 6 and 8.

54. See Louis Koenig, *The Chief Executive,* rev. ed. (New York: Harcourt Brace and World, Inc., 1968), p. 62.

55. Ibid., pp. 62–63.

3

THE PRESIDENT AND CONGRESS

☆☆☆☆☆

Of the many roles which a president plays, his role as "chief legislator" is one of the most visible and most commented upon. The president's batting average in getting Congress to pass his bills is regularly computed. Major clashes over policy are frequently portrayed in highly personalized terms as a contest between the president and a powerful figure on Capitol Hill. And the public's image of a president is frequently based on how well he handles Congress. Much of the history of the national government, especially in the nineteenth century, is viewed in terms of shifts in the center of power between the president and Congress.

The emerging of the president in this role was gradual, but has had its greatest development in the twentieth century. A Jefferson, Jackson or Lincoln played this role with great vigor, utilizing many of the the same tools or techniques available to a modern president. But such activity was sporadic, largely confined to what historians call "strong presidents," rather than being a consistent pattern of presidential behavior. Three twentieth-century presidents, Wilson and the two Roosevelts, played a major part in developing this role into a regular and expected part of presidential behavior. For example, Theodore Roosevelt initiated a wide range of legislative proposals in his messages to Congress. Wilson did likewise but dramatized his recommendations with personal presentations before Congress. Both Wilson and Franklin Roosevelt lobbied relentlessly for passage of their recommendations. All three also sensed the great potential of their office (what Theodore Roosevelt labeled as a "bully pulpit") to mobilize public opinion behind their legislative program.

By the mid-twentieth century, this role was well-established. Even a President like Dwight Eisenhower, who was extremely deferential toward the traditional separation of powers proclaimed that he was part of the legislative process. And Congress expects such presidential intervention. This attitude was reflected in the comments of a Republican committee chairman who told an administration witness in 1953:

> Don't expect us to start from scratch on what you people want. That's not the way we do things here—you draft the bills and we work them over.[1]

Indeed, criticism arises not because of such activity, but because of the direction, ineffectiveness or lack of such leadership.

This development is part and parcel of the decline of legislative bodies *vis-à-vis* the executive, which is not confined to the United States but appears to be worldwide. It is reflected not only in the executive's extensive involvement in the legislative process, but also in the degree to which legislative bodies grant wide, discretionary authority to the executive, and the difficulties confronting the legislature in effectively reviewing executive implementation of policies. On the whole, the twentieth century has been hard on legislative bodies. This century has not spared them from the thrust of change, and such a thrust has often implied "a threat of eclipse, rather than a promise of new vigor." [2] Rather than being hailed as the brightest gem in democracy's crown, in accord with classical democratic theory, legislative bodies have dimmed in luster and are said to be in a state of crisis. Slipping in relative power and influence, frequently eclipsed by a powerful executive, hounded by critics and reformers, legislative bodies are said to be searching for a role to play. While Woodrow

Wilson wrote about "congressional government" in the late nineteenth century, commentators now talk about "presidential government."

A number of factors have contributed to this situation. Like other political institutions, Congress in the nineteenth century operated in a simpler world. Domestic problems were dominant. The federal government played only a limited role in a country under the sway of a laissez-faire doctrine. Even the annual budget was small and more comprehensible than its modern, astronomical counterpart. In this century the demands on government have grown tremendously. The services and programs encompassed under the label of the "welfare state" and the extent of the government's involvement in the economy are indicative of its growth. Not only have the demands increased in number and scope, but they differ in kind from earlier ones: they require a high order of technical knowledge and skill, need continuous rather than merely sporadic attention and appear and change rapidly. Nor do such governmental policies and programs stand alone as they frequently did in the nineteenth century; instead, they are closely interrelated as demanded by a functionally interdependent society. In addition, the center of the stage is almost continuously dominated by foreign affairs where the executive has a well-established advantage. Nor can the dividing line between foreign and domestic affairs be easily delineated.

The president's role in the legislative process is also recognition that our political system is not so much based on separation of powers as it is on separated institutions sharing powers. This co-mingling of powers is inevitable since the political process is too complex to fit into tidy compartments. The whole process is fairly untidy, with greater involvement and interaction among the different branches than the formal powers and procedures suggest. This mingling of powers also provides each branch with means to compel the other branches to respect its position and consider its views.

☆
LEGAL SOURCES OF ROLE

There are a number of constitutional and statutory provisions which thrust the president into the legislative process. In Article Two, Section Three, of the Constitution, for example, the president is charged to give Congress information on the State of the Union and "recommend to their consideration such measures as he shall judge necessary and expedient." [3] But the manner in which a president goes about implementing this power is left to his discretion. To some presidents in the past, it was largely an empty formality, a ceremonial occasion where hoary platitudes could be mouthed. To the first President, George Washington, it was a formal very stylized ceremony, reminiscent of the British monarch's "speech from the Throne." But to others, it was an important element in focusing legislative attention on their programs and policies. Thus as Richard Neustadt writes:

. . . a handy and official guide to the wants of its (Congress) biggest customer; an advance formulation of main issues at each session; a work-load ready-to-hand for every legislative committee; an indication, more or less of what may risk a veto; a borrowing of presidential prestige for most major bills.[4]

It is also a means for focusing public attention on certain problems and issues. Such a message, especially if delivered in person, attracts national attention through radio and television. To maximize his audience, President Lyndon Johnson chose to speak during the evening to secure prime TV viewing hours.

Recently such messages have been fairly general in tone (a "mood speech") or like a grocery list of proposed legislation, supplemented by special detailed messages on individual areas of policy (education, civil rights, welfare reforms, etc.). In 1970, President Nixon decided to also give a "State of the World" speech, emphasizing foreign policy while the traditional State of the Union speech concentrated heavily on domestic affairs.

Such a speech is symbolic of the role the president plays in planning and initiating a legislative program. For legislators will anticipate that it will be followed by administration bills backed up by bargaining and persuasion. Modern presidents have converted the message-giving authority into a legislative planning and bill-originating function. Thus it is one of a number of weapons in the continuing process of legislative–executive relations.

In any session of the Congress, a good deal of the agenda will consist of administration measures. In many respects this is very natural. As head of a vast bureaucracy the president possesses access to expert and detailed knowledge of the nation's conditions. Indeed, most of these proposals do not originate with the president personally or the White House staff. Many come from the diverse departments and agencies of the government and interest groups. What the president does is to select among them, determine priorities and focus attention and pressures on key items. Their submission to Congress is a culmination of a lengthy process of discussion, debate and bargaining within the executive and with external groups to see what will secure the presidential seal of approval.[5]

But the president does not dominate the agenda of Congress as does the Prime Minister and his cabinet in the British House of Commons. In any session, individual legislators may raise issues and propose solutions. It is also difficult to determine where a policy proposal originated. A legislator may have raised the issue first and then watched as it was subsequently adopted by the administration as its own creation. Issues, such as pollution control, drug regulation and consumer protection, were raised recently in Congress; only later did the administration adopt such causes.[6] In addition, before proposals are submitted to Congress, the administration attempts to gauge congressional reaction and to tailor its proposals to maximize its support on the Hill.

The president's initiative role was further expanded by the Budget and Accounting Act of 1921. This law imposed on the president the duty to present to Congress a plan of proposed expenditures for the executive agencies as well as proposals for financing them. But a budget is more than a mass of figures; it is also a blueprint of public policy. As Joseph Kallenback points out, concession of fiscal planning responsibility to the executive in practical terms also signifies legislative aquiescence in executive initiative of substantive policy measures.[7] By allotting more money for one program while cutting funds for another, substantive policy decisions are, in fact, being made. In many ways the budget is a more authoritative statement of executive intention than a president's legislative proposals. It indicates exactly where he is willing to spend funds, unlike campaign or platform rhetoric. Indeed many bills are supported in a half-hearted way, primarily as a form of window-dressing to placate certain groups. The budget is also the most comprehensive plan of action put before the Congress. It provides a focus for deliberation and debate that the legislature cannot provide for itself.

Like the president's legislative shopping list, the budget is a collective product. Almost a year in advance of the fiscal year (July 1–June 30), the Office of Management and Budget goes to work securing and reviewing requests from the agencies and departments. A variety of complex and interacting pressures (both inside and outside the administration) affect the final product.[8] For example, in preparing the 1971 budget, the budget-makers (especially President Nixon) kept a wary eye on the impression the overall budget would make on the Federal Reserve Board. The hope was that if they could be convinced of the administration's fiscal responsibility, they would loosen some of the monetary restraints on the economy.

Congress is not required to accept the proposed budget and generally will make changes, largely cuts in proposed expenditures. The largest cuts will be made in programs that are politically unpopular or lack a well-defined clientele, such as foreign aid. In a few cases, Congress may increase expenditures, such as for medical research or for a particular weapons system. The overall impact of such changes is generally not too great. Thus, a *bona fide* cut of as much as 5 percent is an exception rather than the rule.[9] To individual programs, however, the impact may be fairly substantial.

In 1946, the Full Employment Act was passed which further augmented the president's initiative in the legislative process. It imposed on him the responsibility to propose to Congress measures to keep the economy in good health. And it created the Council of Economic Advisers to assist him in this task.

In many ways, the president's ultimate weapon is the veto—his power to reject measures passed by Congress. Even without any other legislative power, the veto power makes him a force to be reckoned with.[10]

The Constitution is very specific on the manner of the veto's operation. Within a ten-day period (Sundays excluded) after he receives the bill, a president may

1) sign the measure, making it a law;

2) withold his signature, thus disapproving or vetoing it. It is then returned to Congress with a message stating presidential objections to it. If both houses repass it by a two-thirds vote, it becomes law without his signature;

3) he may do nothing. At the end of the ten-day period if Congress is still in session, it becomes law without his signature. On the other hand, if Congress has adjourned, it dies without any further action (the "pocket veto").

The most notable development in regard to the veto has been an expansion in the purposes for which it can be used. Early presidents employed it sparingly. It was seen primarily as a guard against infringement of constitutional rights and limitations, rather than as a means of expressing policy differences with Congress. But with Andrew Jackson, the veto took on a different character. He vetoed twelve bills in eight years compared with ten for all his six predecessors. He buttressed his objections not with constitutional arguments but mainly with his views on what constituted "sound public policy." Since his time presidents have generally adopted his view, what Joseph Kallenback calls the "tribunative" view of the veto.[11]

A veto is a powerful weapon because it is seldom reversed since a president can generally rally more than one-third of Congress to support his veto, especially partisans of his own party. While they may have voted for the bill, they will be rather loath to override his veto since his prestige is now clearly at stake.[12]

TABLE 1

NUMBER OF BILLS VETOED

Presidents	Number of Bills Vetoed	Number of Bills Overridden
Franklin Roosevelt	631	9
Harry Truman	250	12
John Kennedy	25	0
Lyndon Johnson	30	0

SOURCE: *Facts About The Presidents*, ed., Joseph N. Kane (New York: H. W. Wilson Co., 1968), p. 353. Source for Lyndon Johnson only in *Congress and the Nation*, Vol. II, 1965–1968, p. 92a.

The veto however, is more than a negative weapon; it may be used positively by a skillful president. That is, the threat to veto is also a weapon. Legislators aware of its existence, or reminded of it by a threat (overt or covert), may structure the bill to meet actual or possible presidential objections.

A veto, to an extent, is a collective administrative opinion. The president's personal staff, confidential advisers and the affected agencies will be consulted. Thus, in a sense, the veto process is institutionalized like the preparation of the president's legislative program. But the ultimate decision is his.

The Constitution also authorizes the president to call Congress into special session; in actual practice, this power has been exercised infrequently. After the adoption of the 20th Amendment (1933), the need was even less. Prior to that amendment, new congressional terms began in March, but the annual session did not begin until December, thirteen months after they were elected. Since the presidential term also began in March, it became regular practice for a president to convene Congress in special session soon after he took office. But the 20th Amendment shifted the beginning of new terms to January and also specified that the new congressional session begin that month. This provision is also of little significance in a day when Congress meets virtually on a year-round basis. Rather than call Congress to Washington, many a modern president might wish its members would go home and leave him alone.

☆
INFORMAL METHODS

Very few presidents limit themselves in their legislative efforts to their constitutional or statutory powers. These formal devices, in a sense, legitimize a president's overall activities in this area. The informal methods—what Kallenback calls the "four p's"—public relations, party leadership, personal persuasion and patronage are vital tools in his role as chief legislator and often more effective than the formal methods.[13]

The president has vast opportunities to mobilize and mold public opinion. He can easily command newspaper headlines and prime television time to appeal to the electorate for support. The presidential press conference is another device at his disposal. In such public relations efforts, Congress is at a disadvantage compared to the president. In their rivalry for news space, a presidential "belly ache" may command front-page attention and relegate reports of a congressional hearing to the inside pages. The diversity of voices within Congress, as compared to the single presidential voice, may also make Congress sound like the tower of Babel. If the president can use these advantages to create a favorable public image of his policies or at least the appearance of support for them, he will use them to prod reluctant legislators. On the other hand, attempts to translate presidential prestige or popularity into support for specific policies are fraught with difficulties: despite his best efforts a president may meet only indifference to his words and requests. In other cases, such policies may antagonize previous supporters. Nor can such appeals be frequent for fear of exhausting, if not antagonizing, large segments of the public. Some presidents do not have much popularity to draw upon, and thus such efforts are largely futile, perhaps, even dangerous, for if such public support does not materialize, legislators, resenting such efforts as attempts to coerce them, will seek their revenge without much fear of punishment. As Richard Neustadt observed:

> The weaker his apparent popular support, the more his cause in Congress may depend on negatives at his disposal like the veto. . . . He may not be left helpless, but his options are reduced, his opportunities diminished . . . in the degree that Washington conceives him unimpressive to the public.[14]

Another technique open to the president is party leadership. While we will discuss the characteristics of the congressional party later in more detail, several comments are in order at this time. First, as David Truman has pointed out, party is an important reference group for congressmen in making voting decisions.[15] As the most visible member of his party, the president is frequently looked to for a definition and statement of the party's position. But while party is important, it is not always decisive in congressional voting. Rather each party may split on numerous issues reflecting the conglomerate nature of American parties, the diversity of interests and opinions encompassed in each. This diversity particularly reflects the preoccupations of many legislators with local concerns necessitated by control of nominations at that level. Parochial concerns frequently fragment the legislative party, as a legislator finds it necessary to abandon programs supported by his fellow partisans in order to defer to localized or sectional concerns on grounds of political necessity. In addition, a legislator in opposing the president may not view himself as a party deviant. Rather he may see himself as a loyalist supporting the party. He sees the party differently, not in terms of a national concept (as defined by a president or at least the party majority in Congress), but in terms of a section, state or local party. Nor is party a legislator's sole reference group: local interest groups or large national interest groups with which he may identify, personal convictions and ideologies are also relevant.

The nature of the congressional parties thus pose some obvious problems for the president and his party's leaders in Congress.[16] His success depends more frequently on persuasion and bargaining than on direct commands since presidents have few sanctions over erring members. Thus, they frequently have to weave together a majority out of disparate factions, blocs and viewpoints. Nor are their efforts always confined to one side of the aisle. On occasion, a president may even find some of his own party leaders opposed to his policies. Thus one of President Eisenhower's sternest critics on foreign policy was his Senate floor leader, William F. Knowland of California.

At times a president may even face a Congress, where one or both chambers are formally controlled by the opposition party. In six of his eight years in the White House, President Eisenhower faced this situation. Despite his own victory in 1968, President Nixon was confronted by a Democratic Congress, elected at the same time. In the 1970 election, the Democrats retained control of both houses. In such cases a president may try to be both a partisan and bipartisan leader which necessitates a delicate balancing act.

Another technique is the use of personal contact with individual members of the legislative branch. This may take many forms: invitations to the White House, moonlight cruises on the presidential yacht (*Sequoia*), personal telephone calls, visits from presidential emissaries, promises of campaign assistance (including personal appearances by the president), etc.[17] Few senators would rate the attention heaped on Senator Harry Byrd of Virginia by President John Kennedy. The President on one occasion paid a surprise visit to Byrd's birthday party arriving at the Senator's Virginia estate by helicopter.[18] But most presidents devote considerable time and attention to the care and feeding of congressmen, especially those in strategic positions of power—committee chairmen, leaders of blocs or groups, wavering voters, etc.

Numerous executive staff personnel are also assigned to legislative liaison duties, an indication of the importance presidents attach to maintaining a communications system with Congress. Theodore Sorensen presents a picture of the Kennedy liaison team headed by Lawrence O'Brien as one of the most organized liaison efforts in history.[19] O'Brien's aides were selected with a careful eye on geography: they came from North Carolina, Wyoming, Massachusetts, California and Maryland. Among their carrots to congressmen were advance notification of federal contracts, special privileges for White House tours for constituents, material for speeches and press releases, campaign help from the national committee, autographed pictures of the President and help on patronage, public works and other budget items. O'Brien provided congressional names for the President's list of dinner guests, and baseball companions, speaking engagements and telephone calls. O'Brien spent his evenings as well as his days with congressmen flattering, joking and lobbying with them. His office maintained a card file on each member of Congress with personal and political information on him and his constituency. At appropriate moments he would mobilize the telephone, letters, telegrams and visits from party leaders back home, interest group leaders and executive personnel. At the time of a vote, aides took up positions outside the doors of the chamber or established temporary headquarters in the speaker's or floor leader's office.

The fourth "p" is patronage. This method is generally broader than merely job allotment and includes all the preferences the executive can provide or help a legislator with. Actually job patronage is fairly limited in amount since only a small proportion of federal jobs are outside the civil service. And on many positions, those largely within a single state, such as the position of federal district attorney, the decision by long tradition, in effect, is made by local politicians. Another type of patronage is local projects: military installations, river and reclamation projects, hospitals, parks, etc. Thus judicious use of patronage may on occasion help win support for a president's program, particularly in securing a crucial vote. And patronage can create occasional headaches from disappointed seekers.

Considering the variety of techniques open to a president in his relations with Congress, Randall Ripley suggested the following typology:

> presidential–partisan majority
> presidential–bipartisan majority
> congressional majority
> truncated majority[20]

A presidential–partisan majority is one in which the president and the majority of both houses of Congress are of the same party; the president views himself as a significant legislative leader; and he and his congressional leaders concentrate almost exclusively on seeking the support of their own party members.[21] As one example Ripley cites the 73rd Congress (1933–1935) where large Democratic majorities were elected on Roosevelt's coattails (House: 313 Democrats to 117 Republicans, a gain of 90; Senate: 60 Democrats to 35 Republicans, a gain of 13). Where majorities are large, and relatively cohesive, the president can largely ignore the opposition since he does not need its votes. The legislative majority was new and came to power at a time when the public mood was supportive of broad, decisive action. But when the number of dissidents in Democratic ranks increased especially in Roosevelt's second term, and the Republicans also became more cohesive, such appeals were much less successful and little legislation resulted.

In the second case, the presidential–bipartisan majority, the president and his congressional leaders often seek minority support for their legislative proposals.[22] Here the majority party is not united enough to achieve legislative victories on its own. One of Ripley's examples is the 88th Congress (1963–1965). President Kennedy and then after his assassination, his successor, President Johnson, and Democratic leaders worked to hold the Democratic ranks together. They realized that success would frequently depend on securing a number of Republican defectors. And they were able to establish friendly and profitable relations with the minority. Although cooperation, especially in domestic policy, was not constant, and both parties were eager for opportunities to score political victories, such cooperation was essential to some of the majority party's successes.

In the congressional majority, as in the previous two cases, the president and congressional majority are of the same party, but the president is more willing to let Congress determine its legislative priorities.[23] He is content primarily to propose and let Congress dispose. Thus, he takes a much less active role in the legislative struggle. As a result, the party's congressional leaders are more independent of the president having more control over priorities, scheduling and tactics. An example of this type, according to Ripley, is the 83rd Congress (1953–1955), a Republican Congress with a Republican President (Eisenhower). The President's personal involvement in legislative matters did not extend very far. Eisenhower submitted few legislative recommendations in 1953 and a fairly complete legislative program in 1954, but he made few suggestions as to priorities. He relied primarily on his subordinates in the executive branch or leaders in Congress to state his case and mobilize the necessary support. Even when he became involved, he did not use all the tools at his disposal. His public appeals for support, for example, were restricted almost exclusively to foreign affairs. He declined to denounce dissenting Republicans on the grounds that it would do more harm than good. Nor would he use patronage, feeling it did not deserve his attention. On a number of matters such as tideland oils, the congressional leaders, in effect, framed the Republican position and Eisenhower agreed to it. Such behavior was in accord with Eisenhower's conception of the president's role in respecting the separateness and the prerogatives of Congress. But the 83rd Congress did not produce a large volume of legislation. Its performance satisfied neither the President nor his congressional leaders. Professor Ripley suggests that this could have been expected: that Congress is at its most effective (and powerful) when it is working cooperatively with a president who asserts himself as an energetic legislative leader.[24]

Finally, the fourth category—a truncated majority—occurs when the majority party of at least one house of Congress is not the same as the president's.[25] Nor is this uncommon. About half of the presidents in the twentieth century have had periods where this situation prevailed. A truncated majority can achieve some success, if either Congress cooperates rather consistently with the president or if it is strong enough to force his acceptance of some of its measures. As one example, Ripley cites the 86th Congress (1959–1961), a Democratic Congress with a Republican President (Eisenhower). The basic strategy of the Democratic congressional leaders was to serve partisan purposes, to make a record to take to the electorate in the 1960 presidential campaign. Thus, they passed a number of partisan bills and awaited the President's reaction. If he vetoed the bill, they attempted to override. But even when they failed, they created future campaign issues. The President was also in a fairly partisan mood and used his veto, public speeches and his Republican congressional minority to attempt to thwart the Democrats. Such partisanship was primarily on domestic issues; they were generally willing to cooperate on foreign affairs. The President on the whole was legislatively more successful than the Democratic majority. But his actions were primarily negative, defeating Democratic proposals. He would have been much less successful, if he had been pushing positive legislative proposals of his own. Ripley contends that the main point the truncated majority suggests is that to have a productive majority, the president and a majority of both houses must be from the same party. While such a condition does not guarantee legislative success, it is a necessary condition for it.[26]

Another student of the presidency has suggested that despite the tools available to a president for legislative leadership and despite the skill of a particular incumbent, Congress historically has consistently followed the presidential lead in only three types of situations.[27] One is in a crisis where the survival of the nation or its socioeconomic system seems at stake. In a crisis like the two world wars or the Great Depression, there is a tendency for the public to look to the president for leadership and direction and to demand congressional acquiesence.

A second situation in which presidential leadership seems assured is found in national security and foreign affairs, especially since World War II. Even in the instances of a truncated majority, the prevailing partisanship is largely confined to domestic issues.

The final situation is when a president is blessed with substantial working majorities in Congress and is himself endowed with considerable adeptness at legislative manipulation. A case in point is the Johnson administration and its relations with Congress from 1965 to 1967. In the election of 1964, the Democrats made substantial gains in Congress largely as a result of the unpopularity of Senator Barry Goldwater, the Republican nominee, particularly in the House where they gained 35 seats. There were a total of 71 freshman Democrats in the House who were very loyal to Johnson's program. Given such a large working majority and his own shrewdness and drive, Johnson secured numerous legislative innovations (medicare, comprehensive aid to education, immigration reform, civil-rights legislation, etc.). However, such command was short-lived. As a result of Republican gains in 1966 and the President's own decline in popularity (largely as a result of difficulties in foreign policy and urban disorders), Johnson was much less successful the remainder of his term.

But Johnson himself, as a result of three decades of service on Capitol Hill, had predicted this and pushed in those few years with great urgency for his programs. In January 1965, he told a group of administration lobbyists:

I have watched the Congress from either the inside or the outside, man and boy for more than forty years and I have never seen a Congress that didn't eventually take the measure of the President it was dealing with. . . . I was just elected by the biggest popular margin in the history of the country, fifteen million votes. Just by the natural way people think and because Barry Goldwater scared the hell out of them, I have already lost two of these fifteen and am probably getting down to thirteen. If I get in any fight with Congress, I have lost another couple of million, and if I have to send any more of our boys into Vietnam, I may be down to eight million by the end of the summer.[28]

Because of this inexorable attrition in his power, he felt it necessary to pass his Great Society program without delay. And, indeed, the very magnitude of the program also contributed to the decline. No president could ask for so much and work so hard for it and maintain totally amicable relations with Congress.

To some commentators, the immense role of the president in the legislative process is not only inevitable but desirable. Spokesmen for what has been called the "executive force theory" feel the executive should be granted wide latitude for decision-making and substantial insulation from what is termed "legislation obstructionism." [29] In addition, they generally favor "reforms" to ensure and enhance the executive hegemony.

Proponents of this theory are highly critical of Congress, feeling that localism and reaction dominate in Congress and are brakes on national progress.[30] Power on Capitol Hill, they argue, gravitates into the hands of legislators from stagnant one-party districts, men who are not attuned to the needs and demands of an urbanized-industrialized society. On the other hand, the president, as the only official elected by the entire nation, represents "the general will" as contrasted with the partial and parochial interests for which legislators speak.

But such executive defenders do not wholly foreclose some congressional policy initiation.[31] Rather they suggest that if the president fails to act, or if there are gaps at the fringes of policy, Congress can serve as a seedbed for new legislative ideas. In the area of foreign policy, they suggest that Congress is poorly equipped to participate in day-to-day decision-making but can play a role in debating more basic long-range questions and in initiating ideas on the periphery.

There is, however, a body of commentators displeased with the prominent executive role in legislation and disturbed by what they interpret as a severe erosion of congressional prerogatives. Advocates of what might be called the "literary theory" favor a revitalization of Congress to reassert the traditional delineation of functions spelled out in the Constitution and prescribe reforms to bring this about.[32] This group believes that Congress should assert its right to exercise all legislative powers. Policies should be initiated at least as often by Congress as the executive. When the executive does initiate, it should do so in an advisory capacity with proper deference to Congress. While there should be consultations with executive officials, they should be barred from lobbying or pressuring. While advocates of this theory generally view executive power with suspicion, they differ on the extent to which the executive should be limited. Basically, the theory requires a balance among the branches, an activist Congress, but also a strong, vital executive. However, one variant of this school, the Whig theory, would enthrone Congress as the dominant branch in the political system and greatly weaken, if not enfeeble the executive.[33]

They attribute the altered power relationship favoring the executive to the rise of the welfare state, with its vast bureaucracy and the services it provides to the citizenry, to the strong public image of the president and his opportunities for publicity and to the failure of Congress to fight back. Unlike the defenders of the executive, they see genuine value in the views and roles of legislators. While the president's constituency is diffuse and heterogeneous and his mandate imprecise, they contend that the legislators' mandates are specific and precise reflecting the attitudes and needs of their individual districts. Thus, the following assessment of Congress would accord with their own:

Congress has the strength of the free enterprise system; it multiplies the decision-makers, the points of access to influence and power, and the creative moving-agents. It is hard to believe that a small group of leaders could do better. What would be gained in orderliness might well be lost in vitality and in sensitiveness to the pressures for change. Moreover, Congress reflects the social system it serves; it reflects the diversity of the country. There is much to be said for a system in which almost every interest can find some spokesman, in which every cause can strike a blow, however feeble, in its own behalf.[34]

While the advocates of the executive force school also generally favor the socioeconomic policies of the last few years, the advocates of the literary theory are generally unhappy over trends to centralization, social welfare policies and governmental involvement in the economy. They look upon the revitalization of Congress as a means of redressing the balance.

Both the advocates of the executive force theory and the literary theory underestimate Congress. In the former case, they underestimate the contribution Congress can make to public policy, while overemphasizing its negative role. Advocates of the literary theory tend to depict the decline of congressional power as being greater than it really is. Few presidents make such a mistake. Thus, in the course of a TV interview, President John Kennedy admitted "the fact is . . . that the Congress looks more powerful sitting here than it did when I was there in Congress. But that is because when you are in Congress you are one of a hundred in the Senate or one of 435 in the House. So that the power is so divided. But from here I look at Congress, particularly the bloc action and it is a substantial power." [35]

It is evident that Congress does not blindly follow presidential wishes. Considerable executive effort is expended to persuade, coerce or cajole congressmen to support proposals. It still has the untrammeled right to say "no" to requests for laws or money. Congress has insisted on the right, which it frequently utilizes to criticize, amend, add to or delay proposals. Almost any measure that emerges from the legislative mill is different in some ways from the administration's original proposal. For example, the medicare program was, as finally enacted, substantially broader than the administration's version. Infrequently, Congress may impose on a reluctant president legislation he does not want, such as the Taft-Hartley Labor Law or the subversive control and restrictive immigration legislation of the late 1940s and early 1950s. Inaction as well as action can impede a presidential program and also represents a type of decision-making. Even before the president proposes a measure, efforts are made to gauge Capitol Hill reaction and to structure the proposal so as to maximize congressional support and to hold off an unpopular item. Thus, many congressional victories are hidden from public view. Although a considerable part of a legislative session is devoted to the president's program, as we pointed out earlier, the agenda is not totally monopolized by the president. Individual legislators still raise issues and propose solutions, nor is it easy to parcel out credit for a measure. It may have been proposed first by a member of Congress, who then saw it adopted by the administration as its own creation after the groundwork was laid. In summary, it must be said that presidential–congresional relations are not really characterized by any simple superior–subordinate relationship but are a fairly complex pattern of conflict, compromise and cooperation. Indeed, Congress has demonstrated a rather remarkable capacity for survival in an age of executive ascendancy. Compared with many other national legislative bodies, Congress is still a viable force to be reckoned with.

☆
CAUSES OF PRESIDENTIAL–CONGRESSIONAL CONFLICT

There are a number of factors that contribute to conflict: first, the constitutional separation of the Congress and the president as institutions. There is a certain amount of institutional rivalry between the two as they vie for power and influence. Regardless of who occupies the White House, Congress tends to view that man at the other end of Pennsylvania Avenue with some suspicion. And a president returns that suspicion casting a wary eye at Congress, even when his own party is in control. The opportunities for such rivalry to surface are increased by the fact that we do not really have separation of powers so much as we have separated institutions sharing powers. While this blending of powers gives each branch the means of compelling the others to consider its views and respect its position, it also increases the opportunities for conflict and rivalry. In addition, such separation also makes divided party control a possibility, such as occurred in 1968, when one party captured the presidency, another the majority of seats in both chambers of Congress.

Another basis of conflict is the difference in the electoral base of the positions.[36] Congress is the product of local constituencies. A legislator's reelection may depend more on how he caters to the groups and interests dominant in that narrow constituency than on his support for the president's programs. In the case of legislators, especially in the past, such interests were largely rural and small town rather than those of the larger cities and metropolitan areas. The influence of such groups was further heightened by the failure to redistrict legislative districts to reflect population shifts or by gerrymandering districts to minimize the impact of urban areas. On the other hand, because of the pivotal power of large urban states (and well-organized minorities within them) under the "winner–take–all" Electoral College system, presidents have been more attuned to other demands and pressures. For example, the electoral votes of seven states (New York, Pennsylvania, California, Ohio, Michigan, Illinois and Texas) can provide about 80 percent of the total vote needed in the Electoral College to win. Thus, presidents generally have been more attentive to the power of urban and minority groups than have legislators as a group.

Despite the differences in constituencies, party might be expected to serve as a unifying bond, especially if the president and the majority in Congress are of the same party. Although party is important, it is not the only reference group for congressmen. Rather it must compete for attention with local constituency interests, national interests with which a congressman may identify, personal convictions and ideologies, etc. Also each party encompasses a diversity of opinions and interests which makes cohesion on many issues difficult, if not impossible.

The dividing lines between the parties in Congress are likely to be more clear-cut for some issues than others. But even here unanimity is seldom achieved. Socioeconomic issues, such as welfare programs, and the regulation of business and labor have been an integral part of the inter-party struggle in recent years. The president can generally count on greater support among his own partisans for his high priority programs and his appointments. His endorsement of an issue helps to polarize conflict since his prestige and that of his party are now tied to the issue. Cohesion will be especially strong on issues involving legislative organization and procedures. Since party is not always the decisive element in determining how a member votes, a presidential legislative victory may be a result of weaving together a coalition of supporters from diverse blocks, groups and the opposition party.

There are also a number of organizational features of the Congress which pose problems for a president. One is the provision for a bicameral legislative body. To the extent that the two chambers differ in the nature of their constituencies, one may be more receptive or in accord with presidential proposals than the other. Thus in recent years, presidential programs, with the possible exception of civil rights, have been treated more sympathetically in the Senate. Since senators are elected on a state-wide basis, their constituencies are more broadly based than those in the House and may in some respects resemble the presidential constituency. Thus like the president, the Senate collectively has shown greater sympathy to the problems of a modern urbanized, industrial society.

Within Congress, the standing committees are of great significance for the president's program because they provide the money and authority necessary for much executive action.[37] Within the committee, the chairman is a crucial figure. Under the seniority principle, he rises to his position without regard to his loyalty to his party or president. Indeed, since chairmen usually come from one-party areas, they will more likely be influenced by interests opposed to the presidential program, for such areas are relatively immune to the pressures of a more dynamic political order and national trends. Thus, key determiners of policy within Congress are locally chosen and locally responsible. A president may be forced to negotiate with them as if they were feudal barons guarding their fief. The importance of a key chairman to a president is illustrated by a comment of President Kennedy's. During a visit to dedicate a federal project in Wilbur Mills' district (Chairman of the crucial House Ways and Means Committee), Kennedy told his audience:

I read in the *New York Times* this morning that if Wilbur Mills requested it, I'd be glad to come down here and sing "Down by the Old Mill Stream." I want to say that I am delighted.[38]

The committee system also reflects a basic fact of the congressional operation: the dispersion of power and authority to different individuals at different stages. Thus, for presidential proposals to win, they must survive numerous hurdles. After jumping one hurdle, it is necessary to regroup to face another. However, to weaken or impede such a measure is generally an easier task. Control of a strategic point, such as the chairmanship of a standing committee, may be sufficient.[39]

Congressional rules and procedures are not neutral but may have substantive importance and are often decisive in shaping legislation. Thus, the president's success in getting his proposals through Congress may be greatly affected by such rules.[40] One example of congressional procedure is which committee a bill is assigned to. Generally the rules and precedents determine which committee is appropriate. But occasionally some bills may fall in a number of jurisdictions. The decision of the presiding officer over which committee to send it to may be crucial to the eventual outcome. If sent to a hostile committee, it may never emerge from what Woodrow Wilson called the "dim dungeons of silence." On the other hand, assignment to a favorable committee may greatly expedite its eventual passage.

Another example of the impact of procedures on the presidential program is the operation of the Rules Committee in the House.[41] In theory this is the "traffic cop" for the House in determining its agenda. It largely determines the order in which bills will be considered on the floor and the conditions of debate. But, in reality, it has frequently gone beyond the traffic cop function, stretching its powers to the utmost. Frequently as a price for bringing a bill to the floor it may insist that the legislative committee alter or modify the bill to suit the tastes of a majority on the Rules Committee. From the late 1930s to the early 1960s, the Rules Committee was dominated by a bipartisan conservative coalition which blocked key legislation desired by the White House. Thus, congressional procedures can be road blocks to the enactment of the president's program and complicate White House–Capitol Hill relations.

In this chapter, we have discussed the president's relations with Congress in his role as "chief legislator." Attempts on the part of Congress to intervene in his executive domain, through legislative oversight will be discussed in the next chapter. This discussion has pointed out the various tools available to the president in intervening in the legislative process. It has also suggested that while he has numerous ways to advance his program, he also operates under numerous restraints that limit his effectiveness. The president still must deal with a powerful Congress, jealous of his role and protective of its own prerogatives.

NOTES

1. Quoted by Richard Neustadt, "Presidency and Legislation: Planning the President's Program," *American Political Science Review*, 1955, 1015.

2. David Truman, *Congress and America's Future* (Englewood Cliffs: Prentice-Hall, 1965), p. 1.

3. For its historical development, see Joseph E. Kallenback, *The American Chief Executive* (New York: Harper and Row, Inc., 1966), pp. 333–44. Also see speeches in *The State of the Union Messages 1790–1966*, ed. Fred Israel (New York: Chelsea House, 1967).

4. Neustadt, p. 1014.

5. For a discussion of the mechanics of central clearance of legislation, largely by the Bureau of the Budget, see Richard Neustadt, "Presidency and Legislation: The Growth of Central Clearance," *American Political Science Review*, 1954, 641–71.

6. For an example of legislative initiative, see John F. Bibby and Roger Davidson, *On Capitol Hill* (New York: Holt, Rinehart, and Winston, Inc., 1967), Chapter 6.

7. See Kallenback, p. 340.

8. See Aaron Wildavsky, *The Politics of the Budgetary Process* (Boston: Little Brown and Co., 1964).

9. See Arthur Smithies, *The Budgetary Process in the United States* (New York: McGraw-Hill Book Co., 1955), p. 140.

10. For its historical development and utilization see Kallenback, pp. 345–61.

11. Ibid., p. 354.

12. For an example of presidential efforts to see that his veto was not overridden, see *Newsweek*, February 9, 1970, 20–21 in regard to President Nixon's veto of an appropriation bill for HEW.

13. For a case study of such usage, see Nathan Miller "The Making of a Majority: The Senate and ABM," *Washington Monthly*, October 1969, 60–72.

14. See Richard Neustadt, *Presidential Power* (New York: John Wiley & Son, 1960), p. 90.

15. See David Truman, *The Congressional Party* (New York: John Wiley & Son, 1959).

16. For a detailed outline of party organization in Congress, see Dale Vinyard, *Congress* (New York: Charles Scribner's Sons, 1968), pp. 74–84.

17. For examples of such efforts, see Theodore C. Sorensen, *Kennedy* (New York: Harper and Row, Inc., 1965), pp. 348–57. Also see Rowland Evans and Robert Novak, *Lyndon B. Johnson: The Exercise of Power* (New York: New American Library, 1966), pp. 513–25.

18. Incident related in Sorensen, p. 345. The effort was largely futile. Indeed, Sorensen relates at the following birthday, Byrd was decrying the number of airplanes and other costly transportation made available to the President.

19. See Sorensen, pp. 356–57.

20. See Randall B. Ripley, *Majority Party Leadership in Congress* (Boston: Little Brown and Co., 1969).

21. Ibid., Chapter 3.

22. Ibid., Chapter 2.

23. Ibid., Chapter 4.

24. Ibid., pp. 134–35.

25. Ibid., Chapter 5.

26. Ibid., p. 168.

27. See Louis W. Koenig, *The Chief Executive* (New York: Harcourt Brace and World, Inc., 1968), pp. 125–27.

28. Quoted in Evans and Novak, pp. 514–15.

29. See position presented in Roger Davidson, *et al., Congress in Crisis* (Belmont, Calif.: Wadsworth Publishing Co., 1966), pp. 25–31.

30. For one of the more articulate statements of such criticism, see James M. Burns, *The Deadlock of Democracy* (Englewood Cliffs: Prentice-Hall, 1963).

31. See Davidson, p. 30.

32. Ibid., pp. 17–25.

33. Ibid., p. 22. They cite as an example of the Whig theory, Alfred de Grazia, *Republic in Crisis* (New York: Federal Legal Press, 1965).

34. Quotation from Ralph K. Huitt, "Congressional Organization in the Field of Money and Credit," *Fiscal and Debt Management Policies*, ed. William Fellner (Englewood Cliffs: Prentice-Hall, 1963), p. 494.

35. Text of interview published in *Congressional Quarterly Weekly Reports* (December 21, 1962), 2278.

36. For details on the electoral arena for Congress, see Vinyard, Chapter 2.

37. For a detailed discussion of the committee structure, see William L. Morrow, *Congressional Committees* (New York: Charles Scribner's Sons, 1969).

38. Related in *Time,* October 11, 1963, 26.

39. See a discussion of congressional decision-making in Vinyard, Chapter 4.

40. For detailed discussion, see Lewis Froman, *The Congressional Process* (Boston: Little Brown and Co., 1967).

41. For a more detailed account, see James A. Robinson, *The House Rules Committee* (Indianapolis: Bobbs-Merrill Co., 1963).

4

THE PRESIDENT
AS AN EXECUTIVE

The opening sentence of Article II of the Constitution states that "the executive power shall be vested in a President of the United States." And he is later charged "to take care that the laws be faithfully executed." These brief statements are extreme oversimplifications of what is a very complex organization and task.

The executive today consists not only of a chief executive but of numerous departments and agency heads.[1] It also consists of thousands of civil servants (what some have called the "fourth branch of government") who, in fact, do most of the executing of the laws.

Because of the size of the executive establishment, the president does not have the time to supervise and direct the entire administrative structure, even when he does possess the formal authority. Rather he must deal with those matters he considers most important or urgent or troublesome, leaving much of the bureaucracy free to operate at the discretion of its administrators.

Some elements of the executive operate with considerable autonomy. Presidential supervision is effectively limited either by law or by the degree of political support the agency possesses. Thus, the independent regulatory agencies (Federal Trade Commission, Interstate Commerce Commission, Federal Power Commission, etc.) have a legal status which largely removes them from direct presidential control. Other agencies through close alliances with the clientele they serve or through cultivation of friends and supporters on Capitol Hill can thwart or ward off presidential intervention. All governmental agencies are subject to a variety of pressures: the president, Congress, private interests and interests within the agency itself. There is no guarantee that the president will have the greatest influence on a particular agency.

Nor is the executive confined to the execution of the laws. As we saw in the previous chapter, the president plays an important role in the initiation of policy. And so do many of the executive agencies in bargaining with and prodding Congress for particular powers and policies. Laws are also frequently passed in largely skeletal form conferring considerable discretionary powers on administrators. Thus, an agency may be directed to be "fair and reasonable" or "just" in performing its broad task. Thus, the bureaucracy must frequently make choices and decisions that are, in effect, policy-making. To a great extent, this is inevitable. The technical nature of many decisions makes detailed orders not only difficult, but impossible. In other instances, the task of reconciling diverse interests is shifted to the executive because Congress would or could not resolve the issues.

The situation is further complicated by congressional involvement in the implementation of policy. Although we shall discuss this topic in more detail later in the chapter, Congress (particularly its committees) has a variety of weapons to check on what the agencies are doing. And legislators frequently concern themselves with specific details of administrative operations. Thus the president's direction of the executive branch is, in a sense, shared with the legislative branch and this is probably inevitable. For policy-making and policy implementation cannot be sharply divided but are inseparably mingled. Both branches participate in both phases.

☆
THE ORGANIZATION
OF THE ADMINISTRATION

Generally speaking, the executive branch is organized by departments for specialized areas. First, there are the eleven major departments that are included in the president's cabinet:

TABLE 1

Department Date*	Department Date
State—1775	Commerce—1913
Defense—1949	Labor—1913
Justice—1870	Health, Education and Welfare—1953
Interior—1849	Housing and Urban Development—1965
Treasury—1789	Transportation—1966
Agriculture—1862	

* Date refers to the year in which the department was formed.
SOURCE: *United States Government Organization Manual* (1969), pp. 84, 95, 109, 112, 209, 218, 250, 278, 298, 335, 361, 376.

Each of these departments is formally divided into a number of bureaus, divisions, sections and desks.

There are also a number of so-called independent executive agencies. They are so designated, because they do not fall within a departmental organization; in addition, the head of such an agency does not have cabinet rank. Examples are the Veterans Administration, the Selective Service System, the Atomic Energy Commission, the United States Information Agency, and the Environmental Protection Agency.

Another group consists of the independent regulatory agencies, such as the Federal Trade Commission, which are largely free of presidential control. Frequently referred to as "quasi-legislative" and "quasi-judicial," they exercise authority that is not strictly executive in character.

TABLE 2

REGULATORY AGENCIES

Civil Aeronautics Board, 1938. It is responsible for the encouragement and development of civil aviation, and it has economic regulatory powers over civil aviation within the United States and between the United States and foreign countries.

Federal Communications Commission, 1934. It is in charge of regulating interstate and foreign commerce in communication by wire and radio so that an efficient and rapid wire and radio communication service may exist.

Federal Power Commission, 1920. It regulates the interstate elements of the electric power and natural gas industries.

Federal Trade Commission, 1915. Its purpose is to maintain the free enterprise system in the United States by the prevention of monopolies or unfair trade practices.

Interstate Commerce Commission, 1887. It is designed to regulate carriers subject to the Interstate Commerce Act, those carriers involved in transportation and in interstate commerce.

Securities and Exchange Commission, 1934. It is responsible for protecting the interests of the public and investors against malpractices in the securities and financial markets.

SOURCE: *United States Government Organization Manual* (1969), pp. 402, 419, 432, 440, 460, 481.

There are also a number of government corporations (the Tennessee Valley Authority is an example) created to carry out primarily economic operations not provided by private enterprise and organized much like private businesses.

Finally, there are a number of agencies set up as service agencies for other units of the executive. An example is the General Services Administration which, among other things, is a purchasing agent. Another is the Civil Service Commission which recruits employees and establishes public personnel policies.

Agencies are created for different purposes. Some are designed largely as a clientele agency—to provide a voice for a particular set of interests. The creation of the Department of Labor (1913) was a symbolic recognition of labor and was designed to promote and render special assistance to labor groups. Other examples are Agriculture, Commerce, the Veterans Administration and the Small Business Administration. Other agencies are created not so much to serve a particular clientele as to perform a particular task. Among these functional agencies would be the State Department and the Treasury. Other agencies are areal in nature, serving a particular locality or region (e.g., the Tennessee Valley Authority).

This complex of departments, agencies and commissions is

TABLE 3

GOVERNMENT CORPORATIONS

Export-Import Bank of the U.S. The Bank is designed to aid in financing and to facilitate exports and imports between the United States or any of its territories and any foreign country.

United States Postal Service. This is a new agency created in 1970 as part of a reform program to replace the existing administrative arrangements. Prior to this change, it had been a cabinet level department like Agriculture, Labor, etc.

Federal Crop Insurance Corporation. It is designed to help farmers strengthen their financial position by providing crop investment insurance.

Federal Deposit Insurance Corporation. It insures up to the statutory limitation, the deposits in national banks, in state banks that are members of the Federal Reserve System and in state banks that apply for federal deposit insurance and meet prescribed qualifications.

Federal Savings and Loan Insurance Corporation. It insures the safety of savings up to $20,000 for each investor's account in an insured institution.

Panama Canal Company. It maintains and operates the Panama Canal and related facilities and business activities.

SOURCE: *United States Government Organization Manual* (1969), pp. 412, 264, 422, 427, 475 and *Congressional Quarterly Weekly Reports* (May 29, 1970), 1434–35.

sometimes depicted as a pyramidal structure controlled and supervised from the top by the president. However, there are numerous limitations on the president's ability to direct this complex empire, and, as a result, the administrative structure is highly decentralized. Bargaining and negotiation rather than command are almost as characteristic of policy implementation as they are of policy-making.

THE MEANS OF ADMINISTRATIVE CONTROL

Basic to the president's executive authority is his power to appoint officials. Through selection of personnel in sympathy with his basic objectives, a president can exert a powerful influence. But, as in other areas of administrative management, complete authority has not been conferred on him. His powers are hedged with various types of limitations. As Joseph Kallenback has written: "the chief executive may be captain of the ship of state; but he must function with a crew that is not entirely of his own choosing." [2]

Probably the largest group of employees are career employees recruited under civil service regulations with permanent tenure, thus beyond the reach of the president. There are, however, other positions over which the president has some choice. But even here the president may not, in some cases, exercise a meaningful choice. Rather his freedom of choice is limited in a number of ways: such factors as indebtedness for political services, geographical balance in appointments, maintenance of intraparty harmony and lack of eager candidates and suitable skills or talents for the job will limit his choice. Various groups may virtually exercise a veto over choices for certain jobs (e.g., the National Association of Rural Electric Cooperatives over the position of administrator of the Rural Electrification Administration; the major veterans' groups over the post of head of the Veterans Administration).

A number of presidential appointments are subject to a further limitation, the need for confirmation by the Senate.[3]

TABLE 4

CATEGORIES OF GOVERNMENTAL EMPLOYEES

Category	Recruiting Process	Characteristics	Major Tasks	Educational Level
Top management	Appointed from political or civil service ranks; loyalty to administration in power often thought very important.	Relatively unrestricted by "red tape"; good education; much and varied experience.	Long-range planning; protection of values, methods, and personnel of agency from outside assault.	At least 4 years of college is common.
Middle management	Administrative competence as tested by examination.	More devoted to rules of procedure than above; sometimes see both agency head and Congress as obstacles to good agency work.	Daily operations of agency.	At least 4 years of college, almost prerequisite.
Professional and technical staff	Formal examination or selection from list of licensed professionals.	Devoted to work; sometimes only dimly aware of political process and hostile to it; may be oriented more toward professional peers than to the agency.	Technical and professional tasks, such as those of the lawyer, engineer, geologist, accountant.	Usually at least 4 years of college; often graduate or professional degrees.
Clerical, manual, and routine worker staff.	Formal examination or straight hiring.	Some, but relatively low skills; often low aspirations; see government work as "a job."	Relatively routine, but essential to getting the agency's work done.	Most jobs, high school diploma or less.

SOURCE: Adopted from Charles Adrian and Charles Press, *The American Political Process* (New York: McGraw-Hill, 1965), p. 528. Copyright © 1965 by McGraw-Hill Book Company and reprinted with their permission.

The Constitution provides in Article II, Section 2 that the president

shall nominate and by and with the advice and consent of the Senate shall appoint ambassasadors, other public ministers and consuls, judges of the Supreme Court, and all officers of the United States whose appointments are not herein otherwise provided for and which shall be established by law. But the Congress may by law vest the appointment of such inferior officers, as they think proper in the President alone, in the courts of law or in the heads of departments.

From the beginning, however, Congress has tended to extend the requirement of senatorial confirmation to a wide range of positions of rather inferior rank: United States Marshal, district attorney, etc. In addition, commissioned officers in the armed forces also are presidential appointments with the consent of the Senate.

Kallenback has grouped positions into four categories with regard to senatorial influence in the selection process.[4] First, there are positions so closely involved with the president's discharge of his duties that the Senate practically gives him a free hand in such appointments—department secretaries and deputy and assistant secretaryships are examples. Diplomatic appointments, to a lesser extent, fall in this category. The most recent case of a nominee for the cabinet being rejected was Lewis Strauss for Secretary of Commerce in 1959.

— A second category is composed of positions for which the president takes the initiative, but the Senate, on the whole, feels freer to reject his choice—the Supreme Court, Courts of Appeal and regulatory commissions and boards. In 1969, for example, the Senate rejected President Nixon's nomination of Judge Clement Haynsworth of South Carolina for the Supreme Court. Some months later, it also rejected his nomination of G. Harrold Carswell for the Court.

The third category includes those positions covered by the practice of "senatorial courtesy," field services of departments and agencies, federal district judges, district attorneys, etc. For such posts, the senator or senators of the president's party, within whose state the position lies, plays a very important role. In such cases the senator's preferences are a major consideration.

A fourth category consists of appointments, such as commissioned officers in the military or the career civil service. Here the president's nominations are made upon recommendation of the units concerned, and his action and that of the senate are mere formalities.

A logical complement to the appointment power is the power to remove. Again the president's authority is limited.[5] The Constitution makes no express provision for removal of federal officials except through impeachment, but this gap has been filled by executive practice, law and judicial provisions. For many of the top positions, such as cabinet members, an individual serves at the pleasure of the president. On the other hand, employees under the federal civil service have, after a probationary period, certain legal protections of their tenure. Both the courts and Congress have also imposed limitations on the president's removal power in regard to some, but not all, of the federal regulatory agencies, such as the Federal Trade Commission, the National Labor Relations Board and the War Claims Board. These limitations are designed to protect the semi-judicial character of certain agencies.

In the case of removal actions as in the case of appointments, the president's use or nonuse of his authority may depend on more than strictly legal considerations. The maintenance of party harmony, pacifying important figures in Congress or maintaining harmonious relations with key interest groups may loom large. During the Johnson administration, the AFL–CIO vetoed efforts of Labor Secretary Willard Wirtz to remove one of his key subordinates with whom he felt he could not work. The political costs of removing someone may, in fact, occasionally be greater than leaving an official where he is. Some officials have established such a popular following that it would be political folly to remove them (e.g., FBI

Director J. Edgar Hoover, who until recently was almost an American political institution).

Another way in which the president influences the executive branch is through his shaping of the administrative structure itself.[6] Increasingly the president has taken the initiative in proposing legislation looking to the creation or reshaping of administrative structures. For example in 1965, President Johnson advocated creation of a cabinet-level Department of Housing and Urban Development. On occasion, Congress has delegated authority to the president to determine structural details in specific areas. This was particularly true during the Depression of the 1930s and during World War II. On occasion, a president has created an agency by executive order, without statutory authorization, arguing that such authority emanated from functions vested in him by the Constitution. During World War II, for example, some of the war-spawned agencies grouped in the Office of Emergency Management were of this character.

Congress has also conferred on the president the power to reshape the existing administrative structure by executive order, subject to a congressional veto in particular cases. This practice recognizes that the president is better equipped than Congress to initiate changes and that such a need is a continuing one, rather than sporadic. Although such authority dates back to the early 1900s, the most recent legislation on the subject arose out of the Hoover Commission of the late 1940s. This group, chaired by former President Herbert Hoover, and appointed by President Harry Truman made a number of suggestions for changes in the executive branch. It also recommended that the president be permitted to transfer, abolish or consolidate federal agencies and functions. Any presidential action, however, could take effect in sixty days unless either the House or Senate voted its disapproval. This authority, which might be described as legislation in reverse, was conferred on the president, subject to periodic renewal of such authority and still exists today.[7]

A third means of presidential influence is through his

budgetary decisions. Since the adoption of the Budget and Accounting Act of 1921, the president proposes to Congress an executive budget. Aaron Wildavsky has written: "In a most integral sense, the budget lies at the heart of the political process." [8] In each budget are recorded the victories and defeats, the compromises and bargains of the various executive agencies. The size and shape of the budget is a matter of serious contention. Favored by the president in its budget allocation, an agency may blossom forth with a new burst of activity, whereas another agency not so favored may have to limp along at last year's level or a reduced pace.

Another way the president influences the administrative agencies is through his legislative program. Through his program he sets the general tone of his administration, defining its priorities and concerns. Agencies vie with each other to have their programs become high-priority items on the president's program. For example, during the Johnson administration, the Office of Education in Health, Education and Welfare blossomed with new and expanded programs, as the president placed major emphasis on it in his domestic program. On the other hand, the Office of Economic Opportunity (the war on poverty agency), which sprang to life during the Johnson administration was trimmed during the Nixon administration. Some of its programs were transferred to other agencies. Other programs were curtailed, and proposed new programs were rejected. Thus, presidential decisions on priorities can have a direct and immediate impact on the agencies. Also, as a popular leader, the president can cultivate and build popular support for programs and agencies.

The president, indeed, is expected to be a general manager of the administrative machinery.[9] In particular, he is expected to coordinate a variety of different programs and policies, for many of the administrative agencies are animated by a loyalty to their own particular purposes, rather than to overall purposes and policies. Even congressional consideration of policy is highly fragmented with little attention to the total gamut of policies. Thus, the president is expected to provide this viewpoint.

But, as Louis Brownlow and others have pointed out, the president is not endowed with authority commensurate with his responsibilities. His authority over the administration may rest more on his personal influence than on legal authority:[10]

Yet none of these agencies of action, of execution are subject to his management by fiat. . . . Rarely can he order, mostly must he persuade.[11]

The president's ability to persuade is based on a number of factors.[12] One is his professional reputation: an assessment by administration and public figures and specialized publics, largely in Washington, of his personality, personal interests, drives and skills. They must be convinced that the president has both the skill and the will to use his position to affect policy before they are easily moved to action. Another factor is his public prestige: his standing with the general public. If he is high in its esteem, he will be more difficult to resist than if his ratings are low. Another factor is what the president can do for the agencies. As we have already pointed out, these rewards are fairly numerous: higher budget allocations, "high-priority" classification for their legislative proposals, a public champion to advance and defend them.

Another factor in agency compliance is the extent to which presidential directives conform with the demands of the other constituencies of an agency. For an agency is accountable to others besides the president. Among these are Congress (at least, the relevant committees) the clients of the agency, and the staff of the agency (with its programmatic and professional commitments). If these are all in accord, compliance is easy. But when they are in disagreement, it is not necessarily the president's directives that will be heeded.

The president is limited by factors other than his persuasiveness with the bureaucracy in trying to affect administrative policy. Theodore Sorensen suggests a partial list:[13] he is limited by what is permissible (constitution, laws). Another limit consists of the available resources (money, manpower, time, etc.) to carry out a program. Also a limiting factor are previous commitments and programs which restrict his maneuveability. Finally Sorensen mentions the limits of available information. Many decisions have to be made on the basis of incomplete, and in some cases, partly inaccurate information.[14]

The president is also limited by his diverse constituencies. One study has identified five constituencies: Congress, the administration, his political party, his electoral constituencies and their organized interest groups and foreign governments.[15] Each, in a sense, represents a set of interests and powers he must consider when making decisions. Because his decisions generally affect more than one constituency at a time, as an administrator he operates under some constraints. He must frequently persuade the affected constituencies that they will gain, not lose, under his decision or offer some other inducement for their support.

The lofty position of the president and the vast extent of the bureaucracy may also effectively isolate him from many important decision-making points.[16] While he may have direct access to his department heads, the operating bureaus (which in many respects are closest to the clientele they serve and to Congress) are submerged within the department, frequently operating with considerable autonomy from both the president and the department head. Even if he tried to have contact at this level, the magnitude and nature of modern government may have surpassed the president's capacity to be thorough in his supervision and control. From a few hundred civilian employees in the early days of the republic, the government has grown to a staff of approximately 2.7 million in 1970. Whereas, at the end of the eighteenth century the principal activities were the post office and revenue collection, there are now programs for outer space, a multitude of health, educational and welfare functions, global diplomatic and military programs, etc.

Although the organization of the executive branch is, in theory, modeled on a hierarchy; in reality, the hierarchy is qualified by several features.[17] These features, as we saw earlier, tend to limit or weaken the president's control over his subordinates. Each of these limitations is, to a great extent, designed to broaden control of administrative units beyond the interests represented by the chief executive and his appointees to those represented by legislators, the clientele of the agencies and their organized groups, or the employees of the unit. Earlier we discussed the special structure of the independent regulatory commissions as an attempt to insulate them from presidential control. The requirement of senatorial confirmation of some of his appointees is another. In a more informal way, some agencies are so well-endowed with support of a well-organized clientele or have such a great reservoir of public good will (e.g., the FBI) that they acquire a good deal of autonomy.

☆
CONGRESS AND THE EXECUTIVE

Perhaps, the greatest limitation on the president is the role of Congress as it affects administrative policy, for while the president interjects himself into the legislative process, so also does Congress, as the dispenser of funds and legal authority, interject itself into the executive. Indeed, in this day and age of executive dominance, increased attention is being given to legislative oversight of executive agencies.

The term "oversight" is not clearly defined. Often it is assumed to be synonomous with a formal congressional investigation carried on under TV lights before a national audience. While a formal investigation is a potent weapon, one that captures the imagination of the public, it is only one of a number of devices that can be utilized. Indeed, the mere existence of this power, rather than its actual use has an impact. Administrators are aware that their actions may at some point subject them to such an ordeal.

Additional opportunities occur when an agency seeks additional statutory authority or funds. A time limit may be placed on the authority given executive agencies, so that the periodic renewal of such authority provides an opportunity for questioning and review (an example is the Selective Service Law).

At such times, administrators will be called before the relevant committees to justify their requests. However, they may also find themselves defending their past actions or expenditures. They will as well receive advice (perhaps, "directives" is a better word) concerning future policies and expenditures. Some agencies, in addition, are required to submit periodic reports of their activities to the relevant committees.[18] In recent years, a number of committees have held sporadic question and answer sessions where agency officials review administrative practices with them and reach informal understandings. In a limited number of cases, some committees require that their consent be obtained before some action is taken. An example is the requirement that in the case of large tax refunds, the Bureau of Internal Revenue obtain the approval of the Joint Congressional Committee on Internal Revenue Taxation.[19]

Although formal techniques may be important, they are frequently rather *pro forma* in character. Even more important are informal understandings and agreements. There is in many cases continuing contact among the personnel of an agency and the relevant committees (legislators and staff). Such interchanges frequently produce tacit agreement, unrecorded in the public record, that guide national policy in particular areas.

Congressional oversight is carried on by the committees, rather than Congress collectively.[20] One of the major purposes of the Legislative Reorganization Act of 1946 was to reorganize and strengthen the committee system to perform this task. The act also charged each committee to exercise "continued watchfulness" over the agencies within its jurisdiction. But the idea that a committee can and will perform such a function on a continuing basis while performing other duties as well, such as its legislative tasks, is rather like the myth of the omnipresent citizen. There is considerable variation in the extent that committees engage in oversight. And even within a given committee such activities vary considerably from Congress to Congress and even within the same session.

Even when committees do perform the oversight function, members are not equal in power nor equally attentive to their duties. Thus, oversight is, in fact, often exercised by a few dominant members.[21] Nor do such committees necessarily reflect the prevailing sentiments in the parent chamber, rather they may be more attuned to particular interests or groups, thus skewing policy to serve partisan, group or personal advantage.

In their relations with agencies, there are a number of different patterns. One pattern would be passivity, wherein the committee does not, in fact, perform this function.[22] Another pattern would be hostility toward the agency with the committee acting as critic and censor. Finally, another and probably more common pattern is committee–agency mutual cooperation and assistance, almost "mutual backscratching," rather than oversight.[23]

Such a partnership with a congressional committee can be valuable for an agency. The committee can run interference for the agency within Congress and with the president or other executive agencies. Some agencies, indeed, may receive more guidance and direction from a congressional group than from the president. Such ties may further atomize administrative structure and policy and effectively limit presidential control and direction of such agencies.

Frequently, concerned interest groups, who have access to the committee, will also participate in such partnerships. This coalescence of interests or subgovernments, (agency, committee and interest groups)—what Ernest Griffith labeled a "whirlpool"[24]—combines its forces to advance mutual causes. A number of examples follow: the Sugar Division of the Department of Agriculture, the House Agriculture Committee and the several spokesmen for the various sugar industries; the National Aeronautics and Space Administration, the House and Senate Space Committees and the aerospace contracting industry; the Education Committees of Congress, the Office of Education (HEW) and the major education interest groups. Each has an important stake in the preservation and enhancement of a program: administrators seek greater responsibility and power, ways to fulfill their professional, programmatic and personal commitments. Committee members may measure their success by their legislative batting average for such programs and their ability to satisfy major interests in their constituencies. Interest group leaders seek rewards for their members and ways of justifying to their members a continued need for their aid.

A recent study by a careful student of legislative oversight has suggested conditions under which it is likely to occur.[25] The type of oversight he is discussing is primarily that of a formal committee inquiry. This type of inquiry often occurs when the majority party in Congress wants to embarrass or harass a current or past president from the other party. Thus in the late 1950s a number of Democratic committees in Congress investigated particular programs of the Eisenhower Administration. In another instance important committee members may believe that interests important to them (group or individual constituents) cannot be satisfied by routine personal intervention by the congressman with an agency. In such cases, committee intercession is used as an alternative. If congressmen perceive a threat, especially from the president, in regard to their traditional prerogatives with an agency, committee activity in regard to that agency is a possible response. For example, there was renewed congressional activity in regard to the Federal Communications Commission after allegations that President Kennedy was taking a more direct role in that area. Another example occurs when interest builds in Congress periodically for revising policy; then oversight activity tends to occur almost as a by-product. Frequently, demands for legislation result from dissatisfaction with the administration's handling of current policy. Finally, in some cases, a friendly committee inquiry may be designed to forestall a more broad-gauged one by others hostile to the agency. The assumption is that the committee can keep it under careful control and thus neutralize or minimize any gains others would seek through a broader inquiry.

Another commentator on oversight has suggested a number of tentative conclusions on oversight in general:

1. While oversight is frequently equated with formal investigations, especially public hearings, it, in fact, covers a wide range of formal and informal methods. And, more informal methods such as committee staff–agency personnel contact may be more effective and less *pro forma*.

2. Oversight tends to be somewhat erratic. Some areas, particularly those of high political visibility, or of great controversy, such as desegregation of public schools, get considerable attention while other, less visible areas, are neglected. In addition, oversight tends to assume continuation and modification of existing programs or introduction of new programs, but seldom examines continuing *need* or *necessity* for existing programs, or the relationship of one program to another. Generally the committees also seem unable or unwilling to play much of a role in evaluating the general direction and long-range significance of public policies.

3. There is a strong "pork barrel" factor in much oversight, the desire to get preferments—federal parks, military bases, NASA installations, federal money for school districts—for the districts of committee members.

4. Also, there is a highly local flavor to much oversight; as individual committee members use such opportunities to make pitches for or apply pressure on behalf of their own constituents. Thus, much oversight is an extension or continuation of the errand-boy role frequently played by congressmen.

5. Relations between an agency and a committee are not constant, rather they are fluid. They may range from the mutual backscratching referred to earlier to open hostility.

6. Relations between an agency and committee may be better at levels lower than the top officials who are political appointees of the president, who serve for a relatively brief term and whose greatest loyalty may be to the president and his program. But at the level of the bureau and division where there is greater continuity in personnel, where the prime loyalty may be to a specific program and where the president may

be regarded with some suspicion, relations may be very close and cordial.

7. Finally, the committees will be most effective in influencing and working with the agency where there is considerable commonality of interests and priorities between the two and, in addition, where the same groups have effective access to both agency and committee.[26]

Thus, in trying to provide direction and guidance to the administration, the president finds he has competition. Various committees and strategically placed individuals in Congress are doing the same thing. And there is no certainty that an agency will necessarily heed the presidential more than the congressional voices. A good deal of this is inevitable. The tasks of the legislature and the executive cannot be separated into neat, distinct categories; instead, they overlap.[27] Such actions are also part of the continuing rivalry between the president and Congress—separated institutions sharing powers. Since policy-making is a continuous process, neither is content to abdicate at any stage for fear its wishes and those of its supporters will not be heeded. The president intervenes in the legislative stage and Congress (through committees and individuals) intervenes at later stages. It is also inevitable since congressmen and the president have different electoral constituencies whose goals and interests they will try to advance, even if it means transcending normal jurisdictional boundaries.

☆
ADMINISTRATIVE STYLE

After these comments on the president's administrative tasks, we will now examine how several recent presidents have behaved as administrators. A major contrast can be drawn between what might be called the Roosevelt method of a highly personal administration and the Eisenhower method of a highly institutionalized administration.[28]

Franklin D. Roosevelt personalized his role to retain great

power in his own hands. His system was highly unconventional, almost planned chaos, as he threw aside both organizational charts and the canons of administrative procedure. In a sense, he ignored the established bureaucracy to create a new one to administer his New Deal programs and later to prosecute World War II. He frequently made end-runs around department heads and dealt directly with their subordinates. Lines of authority were blurred and jurisdictions overlapped. Formal bodies, such as the cabinet, were largely ignored. Rather he frequently employed free-roving assistants who cut across departmental boundaries to shepherd presidential projects through the bureaucracy. Many of his top appointees were complete opposites whom he played off against each other. What he lost in this system in terms of neatness and efficiency he made up for in terms of personal influence and ability to keep things moving.

An entirely different approach was that of Dwight D. Eisenhower. He preferred institutionalizing presidential relations with the executive. Thus, he placed strong reliance on the staff system, a product of his military experience. He delegated many duties and tasks to his staff. His own role was to make the final decision based on the information and alternatives his staff laid before him. And unless a decision was important or executive officials strongly disagreed, presidential intervention was not even considered necessary. The cabinet was revived as a body for discussion of issues. In addition, the president relied heavily on other formal bodies, such as the National Security Council. Teamwork was emphasized since Eisenhower deplored the administrative altercations that were common under Roosevelt. The main attraction of the Eisenhower system is its attempt to provide the president with co-ordinated counsel. But, on the whole, it appears to afford the president "too little initiative and too little total impact on policy." [29] Rather he enters policy-making at a fairly late point in decision-making, when his area of choice has been narrowed considerably and his dependence upon his staff has become too great.

During the Kennedy administration, the method veered decidedly toward the Roosevelt approach, as Kennedy placed himself "in the thick of things." Like Roosevelt, he placed great reliance on personal relationships unhampered by organization and hierarchy. His brother, Robert, not only functioned as Attorney General but ranged over a wide variety of areas. President Kennedy also interjected himself at almost any point in decision-making from the definition of the problem and the clarification of the alternatives to the final judgment. He also tended to shun the attributes of the institutionalized executive, such as the cabinet and the National Security Council.

As president, Lyndon Johnson blended both the Roosevelt and the Eisenhower approach. He attempted to maximize his personal influence, often using his staff in a fairly unorthodox way, and he frequently sought counsel outside the government. In addition, Johnson often participated in all the stages of decision-making. His own driving energy and frantic pace, as reflected in his eighteen-hour work day, his extensive phone calls, was an energizing influence on the administration. But, like Eisenhower, he placed considerable value on the cabinet and National Security Council. For the cabinet, he had a formal agenda and a cabinet secretary.

President Nixon in administrative style, at least initially, has moved somewhat closer to the Eisenhower system than either Kennedy or Johnson. He has placed considerable emphasis on formal institutions, such as the cabinet and the National Security Council. As an experienced politician, however, he seems determined to play a more forceful role and to be more wary of insulating himself from what was going on than Eisenhower.

Any president's administrative style is a reflection of such factors as his temperament and personality, his previous experience and, to an extent, the precedents of his predecessors. Most presidents are likely to adopt a style somewhere between the highly personalized model of Roosevelt and the institutionalized, hierarchy-oriented model of Eisenhower. It is also evident that a president must generally commit great quantities of his personal energy, time and talent to the task of administration.

☆
THE EXECUTIVE AS A LAW ENFORCER

Another aspect of the president's executive role is his responsibility to enforce the laws. Thus in Article II, Section 3, of the Constitution, the president is charged to "take care that the laws be faithfully executed." In discharging this responsibility, the president ordinarily relies on subordinates. One agency, in particular, the Department of Justice, has general responsibility for law enforcement. But other agencies, such as the Treasury Department, are also involved.

The duty of enforcement also entails considerable discretionary authority. For in applying laws of a very general character, enforcers have to decide what the law means in particular circumstances. This necessitates a considerable amount of presidential direction in the form of executive orders, ordinances, rules and regulations.

The enforcement of the laws is also affected by the general tone the president sets for his administration. Such a tone provides guidance to his subordinates as to how zealous they should be in regard to particular laws. If a president places heavy stress on breaking up big business combines, then the enforcers of the anti-trust laws may institute more legal actions under the laws than if he speaks glowingly about the contributions of big business and of a government–business alliance. In the latter case, the trustbusters will proceed cautiously, tolerating business practices they previously attacked as violations of the law. The type of men appointed by the president to top posts is another sign. For example, when President Nixon appointed Jerris Leonard as assistant attorney general for civil rights, many spokesmen for such groups regarded this as an indication that enforcement would be more lenient than it had been in the past.

Since the effectiveness of law enforcement ultimately depends on the attitude of the public toward a law, the president may attempt to use his position to secure public acceptance and compliance with the law.

As part of his law enforcement responsibilities, the president is regarded, in Joseph Kallenback's phrase, as the "conservator-in-chief of public order and safety," [30] a function central to the very purpose of government. Normally, the ordinary processes of law enforcement suffice to secure these goals. Occasionally, however, direct presidential involvement is necessary. And the president has a number of constitutional, statutory and political tools which he can utilize.

In very recent times, violence to prevent school desegregation under federal court orders has brought presidential involvement to restore order and secure obedience to the law. In 1957, President Eisenhower sent troops to Little Rock, Arkansas, to end disorders and secure enforcement of a federal court order integrating Little Rock Central High School. His successor, John Kennedy, sent federal troops to Oxford, Mississippi, to back up an integration order in regard to the University of Mississippi.[31] Kennedy used federal marshals and federalized National Guard units to back up similar court orders in Montgomery, Alabama, in the same year and in Tuscaloosa and Birmingham in 1963.

From time to time, the president has intervened to deal with violence arising out of labor disputes. Among the grounds on which such actions have been based are that the disorder threatens the performance of a national function (such as the carrying of the mails) or that the safety of national property or the movement of interstate commerce is in jeopardy. On occasion, a president has intervened at the request of a governor to help restore order in a particular state. In 1967, President Johnson sent federal troops to Detroit, at the request of Governor George Romney, during a major civil disorder.

In some cases, the president may attempt to use his public prestige to help restore order. In 1968, at the height of civil disorders in a number of major American cities, following the assassination of Martin Luther King, Jr., President Johnson went on national television to urge calm and a restoration of order.

Following a natural disaster, such as a flood or a hurricane, the president is often asked for help and assistance. Federal troops may occasionally be used to restore order or to assist in rehabilitation. The president may also provide aid in the form of food and special financial assistance. Thus, at the time of a serious emergency, either man-made or naturally caused, the president may intervene to attempt to restore the domestic peace.

Related to the president's role in law enforcement is his pardoning power conferred on him by the Constitution in Article II, Section 2. Such presidential authority extends only to individuals convicted of federal crimes, not to state and local laws and ordinances. The pardoning power embraces the right to diminish the punishment by commuting the sentence, to delay its application by reprieve or to cancel the penalty altogether.

☆

THE EXECUTIVE AS A SOURCE OF POLICY-MAKING AUTHORITY

Another aspect of the president's role as an executive is his power to make policy on his own authority. As a recent study points out, attention to presidential policy-making has generally focused on his responsibility for filling in the details in congressional statutes, or his foreign policy-making authority.[32] The latter topic will be discussed in a subsequent chapter. Yet a president under his own independent, constitutional power also has some policy-making authority in the domestic sector. Although most executive orders are issued under specific statutory authority, presidents on occasion have proclaimed a policy on their own authority and directed subordinates to implement it.

One area in which this sort of policy-making has been prominent is civil rights.[33] For example, in 1941, President Roosevelt prohibited discrimination in the employment of workers in industries having defense contracts and established a Committee on Fair Employment Practices (FEPC) to oversee it. His successor, Harry Truman, by an executive order in 1948 declared a policy of equality of treatment in the armed forces. Another example was President Kennedy's order in 1961 prohibiting discrimination in federally-assisted housing.

The constitutional basis for such actions is based on an interpretation of the executive power in Article II of the Constitution. The provisions involved here are: "the executive power shall be vested in a President of the United States of America," that he "shall take care that the laws be faithfully executed" and that the "President shall be Commander-in-Chief of the Army and Navy of the United States." Recent presidential and judicial interpretations have tended to favor a broad construction of these provisions. In so doing, they have added considerably to the president's reservoir of constitutional powers.

With particular regard to the "executive power" clause, one view is that it is simply a summary of the powers specified in Article II, such as the power to appoint officials (subject, of course, in some cases to senatorial confirmation). Another view, however, is that it, in fact, is a grant of general executive power. And this latter theory has been dominant in the views and practices of recent presidents.

The president derives his role as chief administrator from the clause "that the laws be faithfully executed." Again, there are opposing interpretations. One can view it simply as authority to carry out the laws of Congress—a fairly restrictive view. But another can see the clause as an independent grant of authority. For example, the Supreme Court argued at one point that the president, under this clause, is not simply limited to the enforcement of acts of Congress according to their express terms, but rather his power includes "the rights, duties and obligations growing out of the Constitution itself . . . and all the protection implied by the nature of government under the Constitution." [34] And on many occasions presidents have claimed broad powers under this clause.

Finally, the president's powers as commander-in-chief have also been transformed. In its origin primarily a power of military command, it has been expanded to one of almost indeterminable power in times of war, many uses of which have domestic impact. On one occasion, the Supreme Court declared that such powers and duties were "purely military." During the Civil War, however, Abraham Lincoln successfully cited this clause as the source of his authority for a wide variety of acts, many of which went beyond the purely military into political matters, including suspension of the writ of habeus corpus, military trial of civilians suspected of "disloyal practices" and the paying of funds from the Treasury without congressional appropriation. Ever since that time, this constitutional language has been continually stretched. Now in the days of "total war," when the dividing line between the military and civilian sector is extremely tenuous, this power has been further enhanced.

Although there are a fairly large number of judicial decisions regarding this power, the judiciary has not played an extensive role in determining its constitutional limits. Rather, as Clinton Rossiter points out, the Court has been asked to examine only a small number of the president's actions as commander-in-chief, for most of them were by their nature not contestable in a court but only by impeachment proceedings. "The contours of the presidential war powers have therefore been presidentially, not judicially shaped; their exercise is for Congress and the people, not the Court, to oversee." [35] And the president's broad powers as commander-in-chief have had domestic policy implications.

Of some interest, in addition to the dimensions of the executive's independent policy-making authority, are the reasons for presidential recourse to it. Among the reasons are:

1. Public pressure for executive action, particularly from groups he is courting or on which he is dependent politically. Such demands

are also likely to come from those groups who feel they have better access to the presidency than Congress.

2. Personal value choices of a president.

3. Failure of Congress to enact legislation as was the case with the Fair Employment Practices Act or the desire to avoid a congressional controversy with the possibility of defeat. And in some cases, presidential orders are vanguards of new laws, as was the case with civil-rights legislation.

4. The failure of executive departments to adopt an adequate policy while seeking a goal which can be achieved administratively. In addition, some presidential orders have what Samuel Krislov called the "multiplier effect." [36] Small alterations in governmental policy can have an impact in a wide area. Others, in the private sector, for example, may use the governmental action as a model. This was true, to an extent, with fair employment practices.

5. In some cases, an executive order provides a more flexible, adaptive framework than does a statute for dealing with a problem, particularly one of some urgency.[37]

An executive order, however is not the last step. A great deal depends on how it is interpreted and implemented. While the issuance of the order may be surrounded with much fanfare, it may soon lack any real meaning because no one followed through. Indeed, fanfare may be designed to attract attention and secure political credits out of the order without any serious intent to follow through. On the other hand, a president may make little attempt to publicize an order if he wishes to avoid controversy or fears congressional reprisals against other programs.[38]

Although such policy-making authority considerably expands presidential power, it is not unlimited. Congress may invalidate an executive order by enacting a statute. Some orders, for example, President Truman's seizure of the steel industry during the Korean conflict, may be overturned by the Supreme Court. Grounds for a judicial challenge include conflict with the Constitution, a statute or even the implied intent of Congress. In some cases bureaucratic neglect or opposition may make the order a dead issue. Public evasion or indifference may also largely nullify it. Nevertheless the growth of presidential power in this century makes the executive order potentially a significant source of public law in the domestic sector.

In this chapter, we have examined the many facets of the president's role as an executive. As in his legislative role, the president has a number of tools, formal and informal, to rely upon. And in many instances the informal methods are more important. But, as in his legislative role, the president operates under some constraints. Frequently his powers are not commensurate with his responsibilities. While the president is called "the chief executive," the executive branch is not monolithic; rather, numerous units within it have acquired some autonomy. The president also has to compete with others, especially units of Congress, in giving guidance and direction to the executive. His most effective tool may well be persuasion. And the success of much of his program may depend on how effectively he bends the departments and agencies to his will.

☆
NOTES

1. For a more detailed description and analysis, see James Davis, *The National Executive Branch* (New York: The Macmillan Co., 1970).

2. See Joseph Kallenback, *The American Chief Executive* (New York: Harper and Row, Inc., 1966), p. 387.

3. For more complete discussion, see C. Hermann Pritchett, *The American Constitution*, 2nd ed. (New York: McGraw-Hill Book Co., 1968), pp. 241–43, and Kallenback, pp. 388–98.

4. Kallenback, pp. 391–95. Also see Joseph P. Harris, *The Advice and Consent of the Senate* (Berkeley: University of California Press, 1953).

5. See Pritchett, pp. 344–48.

6. See Kallenback, pp. 381–87.

7. In 1969, Congress approved President Nixon's first bill, renewal of such authority for two years. See the New York *Times*, March 19, 1969.

8. See his *The Politics of the Budgetary Process* (Boston: Little Brown and Co., 1964), pp. 4–5. For the congressional side of this topic, see Richard Fenno, *The Power of the Purse* (Boston: Little Brown and Co., 1966).

9. See Louis Brownlow, *The President and the Presidency* (Chicago: Public Administration Service, 1949).

10. Ibid., p. 90. Also Pendleton Herring *Presidential Leadership* (New York: Farrar and Rinehart, 1940), p. 2. Also Richard Neustadt, *Presidential Power* (New York: John Wiley & Son, 1960).

11. Quote from Richard Neustadt "The Reality of Presidential Power" in *The Power of the Presidency*, ed. Robert Hirschfield (New York: Atherton Press, 1968), p. 273.

12. Drawn partly from Theodore C. Sorensen, *Decision-Making in the White House* (New York: Columbia University Press, 1963), Chapters 4 and 5. Also see Louis C. Gawthrop, *Bureaucratic Behavior in the Executive Branch* (New York: The Free Press, 1969).

13. See Sorensen, Chapter 3.

14. For a graphic example of this, see Theodore Draper, *The Dominican Intervention* (New York: Commentary Books, 1968).

15. See Neustadt, p. 7.

16. See Ira Sharkansky, *Public Administration* (Chicago: Markham, 1970), p. 208.

17. Ibid., p. 72.

18. For example, the Small Business Administration (SBA) is required to make annual reports in which it details the funds expended in the conduct of each of its principal activities.

19. See William E. Rhode, *Committee Clearance of Administrative Decisions* (East Lansing: Bureau of Social and Political Research, Michigan State University, 1959). For a discussion of other techniques, see Joseph P. Harris, *Congressional Control of Administration* (Washington, D.C.: The Brookings Institution, 1964).

20. For some examples, see John F. Bibby, "Committee Characteristics and Legislative Oversight of Administration," *Midwest Journal of Political Science*, February 1966, 78–98; Thomas P. Johnige, "The Congressional Committee System and the Oversight Process: "Congress and NASA," *Western Political Quarterly*, June 1968, 227–39;

William L. Morrow, "Legislative Control of Administrative Discretion," *Journal of Politics*, November 1968, 985–1011; Seymour Scher, "Congressional Committee Members as Independent Agency Overseers: A Case Study," *American Political Science Review*, December 1960, 911–20; Ira Sharkansky, "Four Agencies and An Appropriations Subcommittee: A Comparative Study of Budget Strategies," *Midwest Journal of Political Science*, August 1965, 254–81; Dale Vinyard, "The Congressional Committees on Small Business: A Pattern of Legislative Committee-Executive Agency Relations," *Western Political Quarterly*, September 1968, 391–99.

21. See Nick Kotz, "Jamie Whitten: The Permanent Secretary of Agriculture," *Washington Monthly*, October 1969, 8–19.

22. See Bibby for an example of a committee, Senate Banking and Currency, that largely eschewed oversight at the time of his study.

23. See, as an example, Vinyard.

24. See his *Congress: Its Contemporary Role,* 3rd ed. (New York: New York University Press, 1961). For examples, see Douglas Cater, *Power in Washington* (New York: Random House, 1964), pp. 17–48. Also J. Leiper Freeman, *The Political Process: Executive Bureau-Legislative Committee Relations* (New York: Random House, 1965).

25. Seymour Scher, "Conditions of Legislative Control," *Journal of Politics*, August 1963, 526–51.

26. See Vinyard, pp. 398–99. Also drawn to an extent from Morrow, Chapter 4.

27. See the discussion in Bertram M. Gross, *The Legislative Struggle* (New York: McGraw-Hill Book Co., 1953), pp. 154–61.

28. Drawn largely from the analysis of Louis Koenig, *The Chief Executive,* 2nd ed. (New York: Harcourt Brace and World, Inc., 1968), pp. 163–79.

29. Ibid., p. 171.

30. See such a label in Kallenback, p. 446. For a detailed presentation and historical examples, see ibid., pp. 451–79.

31. For details of the confrontation, see Theodore C. Sorensen, *Kennedy* (New York: Harper and Row, Inc., 1965), pp. 483–88.

32. See Ruth P. Morgan, *The President and Civil Rights: Policy-Making by Executive Order* (New York: St. Martin's Press, 1970), p. vii.

33. For a listing of them, see ibid., pp. 87–88.

34. See *In re Neagle,* 135 U.S. 1 (1899).

35. See Clinton Rossiter, *The Supreme Court and the Commander-in-Chief* (Ithaca: Cornell University Press, 1951), p. 126.

36. See Samuel Krislov, *The Negro in Federal Employment* (Minneapolis: University of Minnesota Press, 1967), p. 5, quoted in Morgan, p. 2.

37. See Morgan, p. 77 and Chapter 5.

38. Morgan cites President Kennedy's fair housing order of 1962 as an example. See Morgan, p. 81.

5

THE PRESIDENT AND THE COURTS

In preceding chapters, we discussed the relations of the president with Congress and the executive branch. Now we turn our attention to the president's relations with the third of the governmental branches, the federal judiciary.

☆

SELECTION OF JUDGES

One way in which the president is involved with the judiciary is through the selection process. All federal judges are appointed by the president with the concurrence of the Senate. And all are appointed for life, with certain exceptions such as the Court of Military Appeals.

In selecting judges for the district courts (general courts of original jurisdiction are the most numerous), the president's freedom of choice is somewhat circumscribed. As we saw earlier, the practice of "senatorial courtesy" influences the selection process. If the senators from the state (in which judges are to be chosen) are of the president's party, they will have considerable influence almost amounting to a veto over the choice. But they are not the only persons involved. As one commentator wrote:

An appointment grows out of the interaction of a number of people with varying and to some extent countervailing powers attempting to influence each other within a framework imposed on them by law, custom and tradition.[1]

Other participants are the Justice Department, White House aides, the local bar associations and lawyers aspiring to the position. Once this informal selection process of behind-the-scenes negotiation is completed, the president can confidently submit the nominee to the Senate and confirmation is generally *pro forma*. A controversy in 1950 between President Harry Truman and Illinois Democratic Senator Paul H. Douglas is a glaring exception to the practice. Douglas submitted a list of nominees to fill several judgeships. The President, however, nominated individuals who were not on Douglas' list. When the Senate considered the nominations, Douglas objected on the grounds that senatorial prerogatives had been violated. The nominations were rejected.[2] Even senators who did not like Douglas were fearful that if they did not support him against the President, they might be next to lose influence in awarding such desirable patronage.

The prominent role of the senators and local groups may mean that a president will nominate men who are not in sympathy with policies he wishes to advance. Despite the fact that President John Kennedy and his brother Robert as Attorney General were strong advocates of civil rights, they sent to the Senate a number of federal court nominees who, on the bench, paid little attention to this cause. Nominees, such as Judge Harold Cox of Mississippi, thwarted whenever possible the implementation of Supreme Court decisions on civil rights, for example, *Brown* vs. *Board of Education* (1954), the chief school desegregation case. For under the policy of "senatorial courtesy," the choices of men, such as Senator James Eastland of Mississippi, were honored. And the considerations governing a senator in such selections are often primarily local or regional in significance and tend to reflect the dominant political and social forces at that level.

Senators and state party leaders have some influence over

presidential appointments to the federal courts of appeal, but it is significantly less than over district court appointments. Part of the reason is that the jurisdiction of a court of appeals takes in more than one state and thus no senator has a special personal stake in who is appointed. However, since the appeal courts are multimember courts, a senator may feel his state has a right to a seat on the court and attempt to exercise some influence in the president's choice.[3]

In many ways, the president's most important judicial appointments are to the Supreme Court. Such appointees because of the policy-making role of the Supreme Court and the guidance and direction it gives to the whole federal judiciary are of major significance. Here the president has greater discretion than he does in his lower court appointments. And presidential domination of the selection process usually entails ideological considerations relevant to a national constituency rather than the more narrow considerations of a senator. When opposition does arise in the Senate, it is based on ideological or policy differences or personal prejudices rather than on grounds of personal patronage.[4] Presidents generally try to appoint persons to the Supreme Court with a political philosophy or outlook similar to their own. Of course, they occasionally make errors in judgment. President Eisenhower, for example, appointed Earl Warren as Chief Justice; Warren led the Court in a series of liberal decisions, many of which Eisenhower did not sympathize with. Earlier, President Woodrow Wilson named James McReynolds to the Court; he proved to be almost the total antithesis of everything Wilson stood for. Presidents may attempt, in addition, to keep some geographical, religious and ethnic balance on the Court. For example, since Wilson's appointment of Louis Brandeis, there has been at least one Jewish member on the Court. This precedent was broken, however, in 1969 when Abe Fortas left the Court under fire, and President Nixon did not nominate a Jew to replace him. When President Johnson named Thurgood Marshall, a black, to the Court in 1967, he may have established another precedent.

TABLE 1

Nominee	Year	President	Action
William Paterson	1793	Washington	1
John Rutledge	1795	Washington	2
Alexander Wolcott	1811	Madison	2
John J. Critinden	1828	John Adams	3
Roger B. Taney	1835	Jackson	3
John C. Spencer	1844	Tyler	2
R. H. Walworth	1844	Tyler	1
Edward B. King	1844	Tyler	1
R. H. Walworth	1844	Tyler	1
Edward B. King	1844	Tyler	1
John M. Read	1845	Tyler	3
G. W. Woodward	1846	Polk	2
Edward A. Bradford	1852	Fillmore	3
George E. Badger	1853	Fillmore	3
William C. Micou	1853	Fillmore	3
Jeremiah S. Black	1861	Buchanan	2
Henry Stanbery	1866	A. Johnson	3
Ebenezer R. Hoar	1870	Grant	2
George H. Williams	1874	Grant	1
Caleb Cushing	1874	Grant	1
Stanley Mattheys	1881	Hayes	3
W. B. Hornblower	1894	Cleveland	2
W. H. Peckham	1894	Cleveland	2
John J. Parker	1930	Hoover	2
Abe Fortas	1968	L. Johnson	1 and 4
Homer Thornberry	1968	L. Johnson	1
Clement F. Haynsworth	1969	Nixon	2
G. Harrold Carswell	1970	Nixon	2

1. Withdrawn.
2. Rejected.
3. Postponed.
4. Associate Justice nominated for Chief Justice.

SOURCE: The New York *Times* (April 9, 1970), 32.

Supreme Court nominees are seldom rejected by the Senate. Recent exceptions were the Senate's failure to confirm Abe Fortas as Chief Justice in 1968 and the Senate's rejection of President Nixon's nomination of Clement Haynsworth of South Carolina to the Court in 1969 and G. Harrold Carswell of Florida in 1970. In the case of lower court appointments, the pressures of an individual senator, at least of the president's party, may be adequate to block or prevent a nomination. But in the case of Supreme Court appointments, the pressures of an individual senator are generally inadequate; a concerted effort by a considerable number of senators is required. And, even in such cases, the effect is primarily negative, vetoing a particular selection, rather than forcing a particular choice on the president.[5]

One of the reasons nominations are infrequently rejected is that presidents are normally careful to nominate men who have not antagonized major interest groups. A president knows that groups that find themselves out of favor at the White House may have strength in the Senate and, in particular, the Judiciary Committee and may carry the fight there. So, in a sense, the most "available" man is one who has had noncontroversial public service.[6]

Regardless of the level of the court appointment, party considerations are the most important. Over 90 percent of all federal judgeships have been filled by members of the same party as the president who chose them. For recent presidents the figures are as follows:

Franklin D. Roosevelt	96.4%
Harry S. Truman	90.1%
Dwight D. Eisenhower	94.1%
John F. Kennedy	90.9% [7]

To reward more of the faithful, new judgeships are also created and existing courts expanded in size. Although expanding population and additional litigation have led to increases, most expansions have come after a party has long been out of power.

☆
OTHER JUDICIAL RELATIONSHIPS

The courts and the president are also linked through the practice of judicial review, the power of the courts to declare acts of the legislative and executive branches unconstitutional, contrary to the basic law.[8]

In discussing judicial-executive relations, it is evident that a strong motivating factor in the Court's behavior has been respect for the presidency and a desire to avoid embarrassing clashes with his authority.[9]

As one constitutional authority has written:

> While the Court has sometimes rebuffed Presidential pretensions, it has more often labored to rationalize them; but most of all it has sought on one pretext or other to keep its sickle out of this dread field.[10]

This policy can be explained at least in part by the fact that the president has "the power of the sword" or immediate command of the physical forces of the country. Another explanation is that while the Court can usually assert itself successfully against Congress by disallowing its acts, a presidential exercise of power will have generally produced some change that is beyond judicial competence to efface.[11]

The judiciary in a number of areas has, in effect, by its own action ruled out intervention. One such area is in the president's conduct of foreign affairs. Justice Robert H. Jackson in rationalizing such a practice of judicial self-limitation said:

> Such decisions are wholly confined by our Constitution to the political departments of the government, Executive and Legislative. They are delicate, complex. . . . They are decisions of the kind for which the Judiciary has neither the aptitude, facilities nor responsibility and have long been held to belong in the domain of political power not subject to judicial intrusion or inquiry.[12]

Despite the reluctance of the courts to intervene in controversies over executive power, there have been some important examples of judicial involvement in defining such power. One example is the president's power to remove officials from office; another is the president's power to pardon.[13]

Presidential actions are also subject to another legal test— whether they conflict with an act of Congress. In such instances, Justice Jackson said:

When the President takes measures incompatible with the expressed or implied will of Congress, his power is at its lowest ebb.
. . . Courts can sustain exclusive Presidential control in such a case only by disabling the Congress from acting upon the subject. Presidential claim to a power at once so conclusive and preclusive must be scrutinized with caution, for what is at stake is the equilibrium established by our constitutional system.[14]

An example of the overturning of a presidential action because it conflicted with congressional policy occurred in the case of *Youngstown Sheet and Tube Co.* vs. *Sawyer* (1952). Because of a threatened nationwide steel strike, during the Korean conflict, President Truman seized the steel industry. When his action was challenged, the Supreme Court sustained a lower court decision declaring his action unconstitutional. Although the justices were not united in their reasons for their 6 to 3 decision overturning the seizure, what the decision did hold was that his action conflicted with congressional wishes. In passing the Taft-Hartley Act to deal with nationwide strikes, Congress had not included seizure authority as a weapon, thus by implication denying such authority to the president. Indeed, Congress had considered seizure as a possible weapon, deemed it a very drastic weapon that should be carefully circumscribed and had chosen not to confer this power on the president. Thus, the Court did not sustain the presidential action since in the words of Justice Harold Burton, the president's order "invaded the jurisdiction of Congress. It violated the essence of the principle of the separation of governmental powers." [15] But such clashes are so infrequent as to be noteworthy when they occur.

The federal judiciary is dependent on the executive to carry out court mandates. Almost any court action requires support from an administrative agency. And in most instances executive officials, whether the president or more generally one of his subordinates, have supported court actions.

One of the more famous cases of executive defiance occurred during the presidency of Andrew Jackson. The Supreme Court, headed by Chief Justice John Marshall, decided that Georgia laws could not apply to the Cherokee Indians within their boundaries. Jackson, who had no liking for Marshall and was fearful of Georgia's reaction, is reputed to have said: "John Marshall has made his decision, now let him enforce it." [16] The decision was not enforced.

A more recent example also illustrates this point: the 1954 desegregation decision of the Court was flouted in many Southern states either through direct interference with the court order or some form of passive resistance.[17] President Eisenhower declined to give moral, executive or political support until finally Governor Faubus of Arkansas used National Guard troops to prevent black students from attending a Little Rock high school. The President then used his office to send federal troops to the scene to enforce a court order. But such resistance to the Court occurs only in spectacular cases involving highly controversial decisions.

The executive also has another power of significance for the courts: the power to initiate cases before the courts. All criminal cases must be initiated by a federal district attorney, who is at least a quasi-executive official. Many important civil cases also emanate from executive initiative. If the executive perceives the judiciary as hostile, it may attempt to keep cases out of the courts.

A president may also participate in efforts to undo a Court's decision by supporting a constitutional amendment or new legislation. In the 1968 election campaign, the Republican presidential candidate, Richard Nixon frequently criticized the impact of Supreme Court decisions, particularly in the area of police practices and judicial procedures. He suggested that some of them needed to be corrected. After he became President, his Attorney General, John Mitchell, submitted legislation to undo the impact of some of the Court's decisions. Earlier, Congress in passing the Safe Streets Act of 1968 had attempted to do the same.[18] Indeed, such efforts more generally originate in Congress than the White House. But if Congress and the president are united in trying to undo the Court's work such efforts are likely to be successful.[19]

As one student of the Court has pointed out: members of Congress and executive officials, including the president, recognize the potential threat to their policy goals which the Court's powers pose and that ". . . suspicion will turn to hostility whenever they themselves or articulate segments of their constituencies disapprove of specific decisions, or when these officials fear that their own policy-making prerogatives are being threatened." [20]

Generally legislative-executive relations with the judiciary are marked by harmony, even indifference. Nor is this surprising. These institutions generally reflect the dominant attitudes and policies in society at a given time. But if conflict occurs, the courts tend to be least successful against cohesive, enduring political majorities and successful against weak majorities (a transient one, a highly fragile one or one united on a policy not crucial to the elements of the majority). And on the whole, the judiciary is more likely to be successful when it avoids highly charged issues and deals with less controversial ones.[21]

☆

NOTES

1. See Harold Chase, "Federal Judges, The Appointment Process," *University of Minnesota Law Review,* 1966–1967, 210.

2. See Joseph P. Harris, *The Advice and Consent of the Senate* (Berkeley: University of California Press, 1953), pp. 321–24. For the role of another group, the American Bar Association, see Joel B. Grossman, *Lawyers and Judges: The ABA and the Politics of Judicial Selection* (New York: John Wiley and Son, 1965).

3. In 1970, there were reports that President Nixon named a Federal District Judge from Tennessee to the Federal Appeals Court for the 6th Circuit in part to punish Senator Robert Griffin (Republican) of Michigan for his role in opposing Judge Haynsworth for the Supreme Court. Earlier there had been considerable discussion of several Michigan judges for the vacancy.

4. For some case studies, see A. L. Todd, *Justice on Trial* (New York: McGraw-Hill Book Co., 1964), also David Danielski, *A Supreme Court Justice is Appointed* (New York: Random House, 1964).

5. Thus, when the Senate rejected Nixon's first nominee for the Fortas seat, Clement Haynsworth, his next nominee Harrold Carswell was regarded as conservative as Haynsworth and in many respects less eminent as a jurist. For example, civil-rights groups who were opposed to Haynsworth and brought considerable pressure to defeat him were even more outraged by Carswell's views.

6. See Jack W. Peltason, *Federal Courts in the Political Process* (New York: Random House, 1955), p. 35. A number of Supreme Court nominations since 1900 have encountered considerable Senate opposition, without having been rejected. These include Louis Brandeis in 1916, Harlan F. Stone in 1925, Charles Evans Hughes in 1930, Hugo Black in 1937, and Felix Frankfurter in 1938.

7. See Frank Sorauf, *Party Politics in America* (Boston: Little Brown and Co., 1968), p. 368. Reprinted by permission of publisher.

8. For detail on the subject and a review of major cases, see Glendon A. Schubert, Jr., *The Presidency in the Courts* (Minneapolis: University of Minnesota Press, 1957). For the history and development of review, see C. Hermann Pritchett, *The American Constitution* (New York: McGraw-Hill Book Co., 1968), pp. 158–74.

9. Pritchett, p. 175.

10. Edward S. Corwin *The President: Office and Powers,* 4th ed. (New York: New York University Press, 1957), p. 16.

11. Ibid., p. 16.

12. See *Chicago and Southern Air Lines* vs. *Waterman S.S. Co.,* 333 U.S. 103 (1948).

13. See Pritchett, pp. 344–51.

14. Taken from Jackson's concuring opinion in the 1952 Steel Seizure Case, quoted in Schubert, pp. 294–95.

15. Taken from Burton's concurring opinion in the Steel Seizure Case, quoted in Schubert, p. 294. See details of the Court's decision in Pritchett, p. 341.

16. For more dtails, see Alfred H. Kelly and Winfred Harbison, *The American Constitution* (New York: W. W. Norton and Co., 1963), pp. 301–304.

17. For a thorough account of the resistance, see Jack W. Peltason, *Fifty-eight Lonely Men* (New York: Harcourt Brace and World, Inc., 1961).

18. For a more complete picture, see Richard Harris, *Justice: The Crisis of Law, Order and Freedom in America* (New York: E. P. Dutton, 1970).

19. The factors contributing to success listed by Stuart Nagel in his "Court-Packing Periods in American History," *Vanderbilt Law Review,* June 1965, 944.

20. See Walter F. Murphy, *Congress and the Courts* (Chicago: University of Chicago Press, 1962), p. 268.

21. Analysis from Robert Dahl, "Decision-Making in a Democracy: The Supreme Court as National Policy-Maker." *Journal of Public Law*, Fall 1957, 286.

6

THE PRESIDENT
AND FOREIGN POLICY

☆☆☆☆☆

World War II transformed the United States from a relatively parochial nation into a major world power deeply entangled in the affairs of other countries. This development further encouraged the growth of presidential power and influence within our system. In addition, while all presidential tasks have increased in complexity in this century, the president's responsibilities in foreign affairs have probably undergone the greatest transformation.

By reason of his constitutional position, the president has a primary role in both the initiation and execution of foreign policies. Although other branches of the government, particularly Congress, are not excluded from this area, they are more dependent on the president than is true in domestic policy. One of the best statements of the president's special position was expressed by the Supreme Court:

Not only, as we have shown, is the federal power over external affairs in origin and essential character different from that over internal affairs, but participation in the exercise of the power is significantly limited. In this vast external realm, with its important, complicated, delicate and manifold problems, the President alone has the power to speak or listen as a representative of the nation. He makes treaties with the advice and consent of the Senate; but he alone negotiates. Into the field of negotiation the Senate cannot intrude; and Congress itself is powerless to invade it. . . .

It is important to bear in mind that we are here dealing not alone with an authority vested in the President by an exertion of legislative power, but with such an authority plus the very delicate, plenary and exclusive power of the President as the sole organ of the federal government in the field of international relations—a power which does not require as a basis for its exercise an act of Congress, but which, of course, like every other governmental power, must be exercised in subordination to the applicable provisions of the Constitution. It is quite apparent that if, in the maintenance of our international relations, embarrassment—perhaps serious embarrassment—is to be avoided and success for our aims achieved, congressional legislation which is to be made effective through negotiation and inquiry within the international field must often accord to the President a degree of discretion and freedom from statutory restriction which would not be admissible were domestic affairs alone involved.[1]

One commentator in discussing the presidential role in foreign policy suggests that "the President virtually determines foreign policy and decides on war and peace, and the Congress has acquiesced in or ignored or approved and encouraged this development." He also suggests that "the position of the executive and legislative branches of the Federal Government in the area of foreign affairs have come very close to reversal since 1789, a change that has been gradual in some degree but with acceleration during the past half-century and breakneck speed during the last twenty years." [2]

But in this area, as in others, the president is not unlimited; he must share power at least to an extent with others. For example, the Constitution allocates the power to declare war to Congress. The Senate must ratify treaties; and the exercise of the general law-making and appropriating powers of Congress is frequently necessary to implement foreign policy decisions. Such divided power may well be "an invitation to struggle for the privilege of directing American foreign policy." [3] In such a struggle, however, the president does have certain advantages: unity of office, capacity for secrecy and dispatch and information. But despite this, one commentator has suggested that "the verdict of history . . . is that the power to determine the substantive content of America's foreign policy is a divided power, with the lion's share falling usually, though by no means always, to the President." [4]

☆
PRESIDENTIAL FUNCTIONS

At the outset, the president is the channel for official communications to and from other nations. He appoints diplomats (subject to senatorial confirmation) through whom official contacts are made, and he receives their reports. He frequently confers with foreign leaders on their state visits to this country. Occasionally, he may go abroad himself as did President Nixon in 1969. In this he was following in the steps of every president since Franklin D. Roosevelt. A number of presidents have held summit conferences with the leaders of the major powers such as Roosevelt's wartime conferences at Casablanca, Cairo, Teheran and Yalta. A new dimension to such contacts was added by the 1963 agreement between President Kennedy and Soviet Premier Khrushchev, establishing a "hot line" of direct communication between Washington and Moscow that would be constantly open. Negotiations with foreign countries are also carried on under his direction, for example, the strategic arms limitations talks with the Soviet Union (frequently called the "SALT conferences") that began early in the Nixon administration.

Second, the president has the power to recognize foreign governments. Such decisions are generally routine, based on who has effective control of a country, but occasionally such moves are highly controversial and are delayed to indicate disapproval of a particular government or its manner of achieving power. Thus, in 1933, President Roosevelt recognized the Soviet Union sixteen years after the Communists took power. Although the Chinese Communists have effectively controlled the mainland since the late 1940s, all presidents to date have declined to give them formal diplomatic recognition. In some cases, recognition may be withdrawn as was the case after Fidel Castro came to power in Cuba.

The president's primary function is to formulate the basic policies of the nation, to enunciate national goals and means of achieving them. An example of a presidential declaration of goals occurred in 1963 when President Kennedy, during the course of a speech at American University, announced that the United States was suspending nuclear tests in the atmosphere. Such a suspension was to continue as long as other nations, especially the Soviet Union, did not conduct such tests. Soviet Premier Khrushchev responded by accepting the principle of a test-ban, and, eventually, a formal treaty was enacted. Most major foreign policy doctrines in American history bear the name of a president or his secretary of State. Recent examples would be Roosevelt's "good neighbor" policy, the Truman Doctrine, the Marshall Plan, the Nixon Doctrine, etc.

The president is also responsible for the daily operation of foreign policy, for dealing with problems face-to-face. Should the United States respond to a plea from an Asian country for arms? How should the nation react to a coup in an African nation? What response should be made to the seizure of an American naval vessel at sea? In doing so, however, the president inevitably makes a host of secondary decisions that can and do set new lines of policy and may commit the United States to future actions. A decision to send military advisers to assist a friendly government may escalate into a major and costly military effort (e.g., Vietnam).

It is evident that no single individual can conduct foreign policy as a one-man operation; he must delegate much of this task to subordinates. A vast bureaucracy, not confined to the State Department, has developed to assist the president. Thus, in many cases his task is to guide and direct this bureaucracy and provide a coordinating force. In cases of conflict among agencies, he may have to step in to resolve the difficulties.

The president's constitutional authority as commander-in-chief of the armed forces also places him in a strong, if not commanding, position in foreign affairs.[5] In such a position, the president is the ceremonial, legal and administrative head of the armed forces. Such authority includes the power to control the placement and movement of the military. Thus, a president may use the armed forces to implement his foreign policy decisions. Among recent examples are President Truman's dispatch of troops to Korea (1950), President Eisenhower's sending marines to Lebanon (1958), the sending of troops to Vietnam by Presidents Kennedy and Johnson, President Johnson's military occupation of the Dominican Republic (1965) and President Nixon's dispatch of troops to Cambodia (1970).

At times, presidents may involve themselves in the direction of military strategy and operations. President Washington accompanied the troops into the field during the Whiskey Rebellion in 1792. During the Civil War President Lincoln made personal visits to his generals in the field and sent orders via telegraph. Franklin Roosevelt spent hours in the White House Chart Room mapping the grand strategy of World War II. During the Cuban missile crisis and the ensuing naval blockade of the island, President Kennedy was involved even in minute details, ranging from the positioning of our ships to the methods of boarding ships that attempted to run the blockade. During his administration, President Johnson at times personally approved bombing targets in North Vietnam.

To a considerable degree, the president's powers as commander-in-chief may largely nullify the congressional authority to declare war. His use of the armed forces may so shape events as to leave Congress no alternative but to declare war. Or it may place the country in an actual state of war, even without a formal congressional declaration. Since World War II, we have been in two costly, undeclared wars—Korea and Indo–China. The congressional power to declare war also seems of limited usefulness in a day and age of push-button warfare, "hot-lines," "wars of national liberation" and Korean-type police actions.

☆

PRESIDENTIAL-CONGRESSIONAL RELATIONS
IN FOREIGN POLICY

Although Congress cannot be an active, directing force in foreign policy, it does possess some weapons which can give it power in this area. One way is through some of its general powers of legislation, appropriation and investigation. For example, the authority to negotiate reciprocal trade agreements, an important instrument of foreign relations since 1934, requires renewal periodically by Congress. One commentator has pointed out, however, that in legislation pertaining to foreign policy, delegation of power to the president to enable him to react to the exigencies of the moment has reached its highest level.[6] Many aspects of foreign policy require funds for implementation, for example, foreign economic assistance. Such funds must be secured from Congress. Indeed, the annual appropriation request for foreign aid is generally an occasion for acrimonious debate and a slashing of executive requests.

The power of the purse is also used to limit the military actions of the president. Thus by witholding funds, Congress can assert some control over foreign policy. In 1969, Congress included in a defense appropriation bill, a prohibition against use of United States combat troops in Laos and Thailand. But since the administration viewed this proviso as an endorsement of its Asian policy, there was no major confrontation. In 1970, a group of senators proposed to cut off funds for retaining American military forces in Cambodia. But no matter how much congressmen dissent from the president's policy, few are willing to deny money when men are actually in combat.

Both chambers may use their investigative power to influence foreign policy. Since 1966 Senator J. William Fulbright and others have used their position on the Senate Foreign Relations Committee to criticize President Johnson's Vietnam policy. For example, in 1966, Johnson's request for a supplemental appropriation, largely for the war in Vietnam, was

TABLE 1

HISTORY OF FOREIGN AID CUTS

(in billions)

Year	Request	Author-ization	Appropri-ation	Percent Cut
1950	5.68	5.59	4.94	13.0
1951	8.17	7.99	7.49	8.3
1952	8.50	7.58	7.28	14.4
1953	7.92	6.49	6.00	24.2
1954	5.83	5.16	4.53	22.3
1955	3.48	3.05	2.78	20.1
1956	3.53	3.42	2.70	23.5
1957	4.86	4.12	3.77	22.4
1958	3.86	3.39	2.77	28.2
1959	3.94	3.68	3.45	12.4
1960	3.93	3.58	3.23	17.8
1961	4.87	4.69	4.43	9.0
1962	4.77	4.26	3.91	18.0
1963	4.78	4.57	3.90	18.4
1964	4.53	3.60	3.00	33.8
1965	3.52	3.50	3.25	7.7
1966	3.46	3.36	3.22	6.9
1967	3.39	3.50	2.94	13.3
1968	3.23	2.68	2.30	28.8
1969	2.92	1.97	1.76	39.7

SOURCE: *Congressional Quarterly Almanac* (1968), p. 605. Reprinted with permission of the publisher.

the basis of a full-dress televised review of that policy by the Foreign Relations Committee.

In some respects, such efforts may be directed as much at public opinion (at least the attentive public and key opinion leaders) as they are at the president. The hope is to create a climate of opinion which negatively restrains or limits presidential conduct or positively permits him to make certain moves without serious political costs.

The Senate, at least, is also associated with foreign policy through the treaty-making power. The Constitution provides that the president "shall have the power, by and with the advice and consent of the Senate to make treaties, provided two-thirds of the Senators present concur." The founding fathers visualized the Senate as a kind of council with which the president would sit and from which he would receive advice during the actual negotiation of a treaty. But such a practice was not followed after George Washington's presidency.[7] Treaties are, in effect, negotiated by the executive, though key congressional leaders are consulted and may be included in the delegation.

The constitutional requirement of two-thirds support means the president must not only hold his own partisans, but secure opposition votes as well. For example, President Woodrow Wilson's failure to attract significant Republican votes denied United States membership in the League of Nations at the end of World War I. In more recent times, the 1963 nuclear test-ban treaty could never have passed without Republican votes and the skill of the late Senate Republican leader, Everett Dirksen of Illinois.

Describing senatorial consideration of treaties, John Hay, a one-time secretary of State wrote: "a treaty entering the Senate is like a bull going into the arena. No one can say just how or when the final blow will fall—but one thing is certain, it will never leave the arena alive." [8] This view is rather exaggerated, but the Senate can have an impact through the ratification process. The Senate can defeat the treaty entirely, although this happens only in a small number of cases. It may approve the treaty unconditionally, or it may approve the treaty with amendments or attach reservations that do not alter the content of the treaty but do qualify the obligation assumed by the United States.

Depending on the nature of the treaty, Congress as a whole may be involved at another step. Some treaties are not self-executing; that is, they require implementing legislation to give them effect as domestic law. A treaty which involved the appropriating of money by Congress would be of this character. It would require a separate action—the passage of a bill by Congress to provide the necessary funds.

TABLE 2

COMPILATION OF SENATE ACTION ON TREATIES, 1789–1963

	Number	Percent
Treaties approved unconditionally	944	69
Approved with amendments and reservations	252	18.4
No action or withdrawn	118	8.6
Rejected	15	1.1
Pending	29	2.1
Submitted, but no action requested	10	.7
Total	1368	

SOURCE: The New York *Times* (August 25, 1963).

Not all agreements with foreign governments, however, take the form of a treaty. Some take the form of an "executive agreement," which need not be submitted to the Senate for ratification. Many deal with relatively minor matters—for example, financial claims of Americans against foreign governments. Another example is the manner of enforcement of custom or immigration laws. Executive agreements on such fairly routine matters are a rather common part of the administration of laws in situations where the United States government and a foreign government have a common interest.

Some executive agreements deal with matters of considerable importance. For example, the Nixon administration negotiated an executive agreement with Spain providing for continued American use of a Polaris submarine base and two air bases. It also provided for economic and military assistance to Spain. This agreement was actually a renewal of a relationship established during the Eisenhower administration.

Such authority of the executive to make international agreements is derived from the president's power as commander-in-chief or in his position as the sole organ of international relations. In some cases, however, the president may be authorized by law or by treaty to enter into such agreements to give effect to their provisions. One of the best examples is the Reciprocal

TABLE 3

TREATIES CONSIDERED BY THE SENATE IN 1969 AND ACTION

Treaties	Senate Committee Action	Senate Floor Action	Final Outcome
1. Treaty on non-proliferation of nuclear weapons. 2/5/69	favorable	favorable	favorable
2. Paris Convention for the protection of industrial property. 3/12/69	favorable	—	—
3. Convention establishing the World Intellectual Property Organization. 3/12/69	favorable	—	—
4. Agreement between the United States and Canada for additional temporary diversions of the Niagara River for power purposes. 3/14/69	favorable	favorable	favorable
5. Two radio broadcasting agreements with the United Mexican states. 3/35/69	favorable	favorable	favorable
6. Convention on conduct of fishing operations in the North Atlantic. 4/16/69	favorable	favorable	favorable
7. Consular convention dealing with functions, privileges and immunities of consular officers. 10/8/69	favorable	favorable	—
8. Convention relating to the estate and inheritance tax with the Netherlands for the purpose of avoiding double taxation. 10/13/69	favorable	—	—
9. Agreements dealing with adjustments in flood control payments to Canada, resulting from early completion of two projects on the Columbia River. 10/14/69	favorable	favorable	—
10. Geneva Protocol of 1925 which prohibits the first use in war of "asphyxiating, poisonous, or other gases and bacteriological methods of warfare." 11/25/69	—	—	—
11. Vienna Convention on consular relations and optional protocol concerning the compulsory settlement of disputes. 5/5/69	favorable	favorable	favorable

SOURCE: *Congressional Quarterly Almanac* (1969), p. 118.

Trade Agreement Act of 1934. Under this law, the president may make executive agreements providing for tariff concessions or reduction of other trade restrictions. On occasion the president may enter into an executive agreement with the proviso that it shall be binding only when Congress adopts implementing legislation. An example is the St. Lawrence Seaway Act of 1954 which was designed to implement an executive agreement with the Canadian government to construct navigational improvements and power facilities on the St. Lawrence River.

Attempts to distinguish between treaties and executive agreements are difficult. There seems to be no essential difference in terms of the subject matters they can deal with. Efforts to distinguish the legal effects of the two have also been generally unsuccessful. The basic difference is in their making: treaties require the concurrence of the Senate; executive agreements do not. The president thus has a choice. And in a greater number of cases, he has resorted to the executive agreement. Certainly, in some cases, such an approach was utilized to avoid possible dangers in sending a treaty to the Senate.

In some respects, the congressional role in foreign affairs is similar to Walter Bagehot's classic definition of the role of the British monarch: "the right to be consulted, the right to encourage, the right to warn." Presidents have generally felt obligated to keep Congress informed about a critical situation or problem and to seek its cooperation in support of a course of action. Frequently a president will seek the opinions of congressmen, singly or collectively. But the makeup of such groups is rather fluid, depending on the issue and the position occupied by the congressman. Such a course of action has certain advantages for a president. Congressional support strengthens his position by giving the impression that he speaks for a united nation. It also commits Congress to support that policy with the necessary resources, particularly financial.

On a number of occasions, presidents have for these reasons sought congressional endorsement even for the movement of military forces, although such authority clearly falls within their power as commander-in-chief. In 1955, for example, President Eisenhower asked for a resolution of support for use of American forces, if necessary, to repel a possible Chinese Communist attack on the Chinese Nationalist bases on Formosa and several off-shore islands. In this specific case, another reason was the memory of the congressional attacks on President Truman for his unilateral decision in 1950 to commit military forces to the defense of South Korea when it was attacked by its Communist neighbor, North Korea. Again, in 1957, President Eisenhower sought congressional endorsement of possible military moves in the Middle East after an uprising occurred in Lebanon. Such precedents were utilized by President Johnson in 1964. After an alleged North Vietnamese attack on several American destroyers, the president asked for congressional support to strengthen his hand. With little dissent, Congress adopted the "Tonkin Gulf Resolution," supporting the president in taking all necessary measures to repel any armed attack against the forces of the United States and to prevent further aggression.[9] Subsequently the president relied on this resolution as partial justification for a tremendous increase in military operations in South Vietnam and the bombing of North Vietnam. Thus, in effect, the resolution served as a functional declaration of war. A number of senators were critical of the president's use of the resolution and felt they had been manipulated into a situation where they had to support it or give an impression of national disunity.

Some congressmen have complained about these requests. Such requests, they contend, generally come after steps have already been taken which commit the country to a course of action. At that point, Congress has little choice but to either embrace such requests or create an impression of disunity, thus possibly undermining the whole effort. Representative Henry Reuss of Wisconsin illustrated this dilemma with a story about a bartender and the owner of a saloon.[10] The bartender calls the owner to ask if a patron is good for a drink on credit:

> Proprietor: "Has he had it?"
> Bartender: "He has."
> Proprietor: "He is."

Congress, like the saloon owner, is in effect confronted by a *fait accompli* and may have little real choice in the matter.

Another way in which congressional criticism may be muted is through a bipartisan foreign policy.[11] Such a concept has a hallowed position in American political folklore. Its basic premise is that in regard to foreign policy, politics should end "at the water's edge," and that it should be the policy of all the people, regardless of partisanship. But the practical effect of such a policy has generally been to increase the power of the president and reduce congressional capacity to act meaningfully on foreign policy. A skillful president, by consulting with opposition leaders or appointing them to office, attempts to implicate or tie them to a particular decision. But frequently such consultation is rather *pro forma* or comes too late to permit an examination of various alternatives. An extreme example occurred during the Cuban missile crisis. President Kennedy consulted bipartisan congressional leaders at five in the evening and made his national address at seven. Another problem is that with our type of political parties there is no clear-cut answer as to who speaks for the party, since it does not control the White House. Rather the president decides with whom he will confer or whom he will appoint to office. Such individuals may merely represent themselves or a faction of the other party. But if a member of that party criticizes the president, the onus of partisanship is on him. There is no guarantee that the president himself is being nonpartisan. In foreign policy, as in farm or labor policy, a president can be highly partisan.

As an example of a warning to the president, one can cite the "national commitments resolution" passed by the Senate in June 1969. Passed by a vote of 70–16, the resolution stated:

Resolved that a national commitment for the purpose of his resolution means the use of the armed forces on foreign territory, or a promise to assist a foreign country, government or people by the use of the armed forces or financial resources of the United States, either immediately or upon the happening of certain events, and

That it is the sense of the Senate that a national commitment by the United States results only from affirmative action taken by the legislative and executive branches of the United States Government by means of a treaty, statute, or concurrent resolution of both houses of Congress specifically providing for such commitment.[12]

While the resolution is not binding upon the executive, the strong support for it in the Senate was a form of pressure on the administration to give greater weight to congressional opinion and sentiments in foreign policy-making. Although passed during the Nixon administration, the resolution, if anything, was directed at the Johnson administration and its entanglement in Vietnam. It was described as an attempt to redress a "constitutional imbalance" that had developed over the last fifty years as the executive had acquired more power over foreign policy. It is doubtful that a mere resolution could achieve such a goal. Indeed, such an imbalance may be irreversible, but it is a sign that the president should proceed with more caution and pay more deference to congressional prerogatives.

An earlier episode also illustrates this warning function of Congress. In 1950, President Truman sent four American army divisions to Western Europe to strengthen the forces of the North Atlantic Alliance. The president relied on his powers as commander-in-chief and did not seek formal congressional approval. This action caused an uproar in Congress and stimulated the so-called "Great Debate" of early 1951.[13] One resolution proposed that no additional troops be sent outside the United States or its possessions without prior authorization of Congress. It would also have denied the use of any current or future appropriations to maintain troops sent without congressional consent. The final resolution that passed was much milder in tone. It suggested that the president consult with the appropriate congressional committees before any future deployment of troops and that the president keep Congress informed on the military efforts of the NATO powers. Although the final action was less than a direct challenge to the president, it probably induced the next president, Eisenhower, to collaborate more closely with Congress in foreign affairs.

Congress may also occasionally play a role in setting the tone and limits of some policies.[14] One example is the case of our China policy in the 1950s and 1960s. Some congressmen took the lead in solidifying a consensus on a rigid policy toward Communist China including nonrecognition. Any presidential attempt to change this policy met stiff resistance including angry speeches, petition drives and, even more important, threats of retaliation on a whole range of matters over which Congress has jurisdiction. Thus presidents concluded that the political costs of attempting to change the policy were too great.

In conclusion, one commentator in summing up the congressional role suggests that Congress has little direct control over foreign policy and can take few initiatives. It participates only fitfully in its actual formulation. As a whole, it can criticize, block, amend or add to. But only occasionally can it force executive attention to a need for change in existing policies. And rarely can it develop and secure public approval for a policy of its own.[15] Indeed, Congress is not a monolithic body. Seldom, if ever, is there unanimity on a policy. A skillful president can capitalize on such divisiveness to augment his own power and sustain his own policies.

☆

THE FOREIGN POLICY-MAKING PROCESS

According to Roger Hilsman, the foreign policy-making process can be viewed as a series of concentric circles.[16] The innermost circle consists of the president and a few key aides as well as top decision-makers in the State and Defense Departments (the secretary of State, Defense and the assistant secretaries who bear responsibility for the particular problem) and the director of the Central Intelligence Agency. Indeed, some matters may not go beyond this inner circle for decision. One example was a decision in September 1962 on how many U-2 flights would be made over Cuba and how many around its periphery. But even in this circle as Hilsman points out, the decision is "political," the "closed politics" of secret decision-making, because of the conflicting interests among the participants.[17] In addition, decisions made in this circle take into account, to an extent, the possible effects, reactions and repercussions in the other circles as well. Beyond this circle is one made of other departments and agencies and other levels of departments already involved. Even though the debate may remain largely secret, it quickly expands or spills over into this circle. One of the reasons this takes place is that the original participants use the decisions of others to buttress or support their own positions.

The next circle is the public one involving Congress, the press, interest groups and at least some segments of the general public. However, Hilsman distinguishes between decisions which become public, in the sense of awareness and visibility, but which never really involve elements of the public circle in the actual decision-making and those decisions in which at least some elements of the public circle do become involved in decision-making.[18] An example of the former would be the Cuban missile crisis between the United States and the Soviet Union. During this awesome confrontation, the public watched and waited to see what the eventual outcome would be, while the actual life-or-death decisions were made by a small number of men.[19] An example of the latter would be some aspects of American policy in Vietnam or American nonrecognition of Communist China.

Earlier, we discussed the role of Congress in foreign policy decision-making. Here we will briefly examine the role of the general public. As a number of students of public opinion have suggested, there is not one public but many. For each policy area there is likely to be an informed and interested group, an "attentive public"—one for agricultural policy, another for Latin America, one for Asian policy, etc. And while such publics may overlap and vary in size over time, they seldom, if ever, include the entire population. For many people foreign policy issues, even more so than domestic issues, are not relevant to their immediate experiences and knowledge. One commentator has cited the great dependence of public interest in foreign affairs on very dramatic and threatening events and the great pull of domestic, private affairs even during an international crisis as an example of public disinterest.[20] In addition, some of the reference groups to which an individual normally turns for guidance to help him pattern key attitudes, such as party affiliation, are of less help in foreign than domestic affairs.[21] Finally, the veil of secrecy over wide areas makes it difficult for the general public, even if it wants to, to acquire information and make meaningful criticisms.

This lack of knowledge and cues as well as the sporadic nature of the public's interest, frequently produces a reaction to foreign affairs which is "one of mood, unstable and subject to manipulation." [22] Also when debate does take place in the public arena, issues are greatly oversimplified. But since attention is easily diverted, the alternatives must be pictured as simple and clear-cut—the "good guys" versus the "bad guys," for example. Frequently the level of such debate is reduced to folk maxims such as "charity begins at home," "let them paddle their own canoe," etc.

As a result the general public frequently prefers to look to others who are felt to be more knowledgeable and informed than they are in foreign affairs to make the decisions. And the figure they turn to or favor is the president more than any other participant. Thus, the general public gives the president considerable leeway in what he does in foreign affairs. Such leeway, which is considerable in ordinary times, tends to substantially increase in a crisis.

A recent study suggested that public opinion, in general, tends to mirror the many-sided policy debate in Washington rather than being one-sided, and therefore clearly favoring a particular position.[23] Thus, rather than limiting the president, public opinion may be permissive, providing some support for any position he chooses to take. Thus a president, or another public official for that matter, can find support for his particular position in the public which he uses to justify and legitimize his position. This same study found that, at least in regard to one issue, the president's support increased, at least temporarily, no matter what he did, as long as he did something.[24] And certainly the president is in a key position to crystallize attitudes for or against a particular policy.

Even in the area of foreign policy, however, the president is not unlimited. He is affected, as are other officials, by the rule of anticipated reactions. He must be constantly concerned about the potential reaction of the public, for there is always a possibility that some of his policies may encounter an adverse reaction and pose political dangers. There may also be certain imprecisely defined limits within which foreign policy must be formulated. Thus, V. O. Key suggested that there are certain types of basic opinions that possess a high degree of stability.[25] One, he suggests, is loyalty to the nation and its obverse of hostility to those who threaten the nation. Such opinions may also include fairly stable attitudes toward individual countries viewing some sympathetically and others in a hostile or suspicious way. These attitudes may set up what Key calls a system of dikes within which normal actions of policy may occur without causing popular reaction.

In regard to interest groups, opinions are easier to discern in domestic affairs because there is a stable structure of interest groups covering most matters of concern—farm, business, labor, veterans, professions, etc. But in foreign policy the interest group structure is "weak, unstable and thin rather than dense."[26] In many matters, it is difficult to think of a well-known interest group. Some ephemeral groups arise from time to time for or against particular policies; they quickly disappear with the solution of the problem. The most prestigious groups like the Council on Foreign Relations are very heterogeneous and cannot take decisive positions on controversial issues. In many ways, the strongest groups may be ethnic ones.[27]

Such groups, however, are most effective when they are narrowly focused and fairly intense; thus on many issues they do not limit the president. And at times ethnic groups conflict on significant issues. One way such groups may influence the president is not to dictate the policy decision, but to affect his agenda.[28] Since there are many policy issues competing for his attention, group activity may pay off in directing presidential attention to an issue. As a result of such attention a president may seek alternative sources of advice, and he may develop different preferences and priorities.

☆

ADMINISTRATION OF FOREIGN AFFAIRS

As was pointed out earlier, the president is charged with the conduct of foreign affairs, but it is evident that he cannot do the job alone, and especially he cannot handle all the day-to-day details. A variety of departments, agencies and offices have been set up to assist him. At the center, in many respects, is the Department of State. Subject to presidential direction and control, the department performs a number of functions:

1. the gathering of information for the President and other officials, including Congress, to keep up on the effects of our policies and events in other countries;

2. representing the United States abroad through the Foreign Service and in international organizations;

3. serving as a major executive agency for implementing foreign policy;

4. helping to interpret the United States to governments and private individuals abroad.[29]

The office of secretary of State is a very prestigious one in American history. Some presidents have delegated considerable authority to their appointees. Such was the case with President Eisenhower and his long-time secretary, John Foster Dulles. Indeed, Dulles enjoyed almost unparalleled power in negotiation and policy formation and as a national spokesman. Other presidents have acted almost as their own secretaries of State (Kennedy, for example). Indeed, given the high priority of foreign policy, it is difficult for a president not to become directly and frequently involved. Nor is presidential attention limited to major items. Given the fact that small problems can potentially have great effects, a president may devote many hours and days to what appears to the casual onlooker as very petty matters, undeserving of his attention.

But foreign policy has too many facets to be confined to the narrow confines of a single department. Various sectors of the sprawling bureaucracy help administer the diplomatic, military, economic, scientific and psychological aspects of foreign policy. An especially important role is played by the Defense Department. At times, its role has even appeared to eclipse that of the State Department. In addition, the complex interrelationship of foreign and domestic policy in the modern world means that the policies of a wide array of departments have some relationship to foreign policy, for example, the Department of Agriculture and its efforts to dispose of farm surpluses overseas. Such efforts may interfere with established trading relationships of other countries. Another example are our civil-rights policies and their impact on our relationships with many of the new African nations.

Presidents have also relied on their own White House staff to maximize their personal involvement in foreign affairs. President Kennedy placed great reliance on his special assistant for national security, McGeorge Bundy, and a small staff to oversee development in foreign policy and national security.[30] From time to time, presidents have also appointed special agents for missions abroad. For example, Richard Nixon as president-elect sent former Governor William Scanton of Pennsylvania to the Middle East to make an evaluation of American policy in that area. Earlier, President Johnson sent then Attorney-General Robert Kennedy to Indonesia to persuade President Sukarno not to attack Malaysia. Such representatives bear considerable prestige as personal agents of the president.

In addition, they may be more attuned to his thinking and policies than the Foreign Service personnel in the field.

A president also finds that such departments and agencies pose some problems: their abilities and the value of their judgments, the reliability of their information and their willingness to implement his policies are examples.

Despite the vast array of helpers, the ultimate decision on major issues is the president's. Since some decisions are life-or-death decisions, there is a tremendous psychological burden imposed on any president. This is especially the case, because he knows that his information is always incomplete, the full consequences of his actions not notably predictable and no perfect solution at hand. Although the president has more power in foreign than domestic affairs, he is, as we have seen, not unlimited. Rather he operates under a variety of constraints. While as a pivotal figure in world affairs, he is more powerful than presidents in an earlier age, he is also circumscribed in ways unknown to his predecessors.

NOTES

1. See *United States* vs. *Curtis-Wright Export Corporation*, 299 U.S. 304 (1936); also reprinted in Robert S. Hirschfield, ed. *The Power of the Presidency* (New York: Atherton Press, 1968), pp. 170–75, quote appears on p. 173.

2. See testimony of Professor Ruhl J. Bartlett before Senate Foreign Relations Committee reported in the New York *Times*, May 18, 1970.

3. Edward S. Corwin, *The President: Office and Powers*, 4th ed. (New York: New York University Press, 1957), p. 171.

4. Ibid., p. 171.

5. For a broad discussion of the various facets of this role, see Joseph E. Kallenback, *The American Chief Executive* (New York: Harper and Row, Inc., 1966), Chapter 16. Also see J. Malcolm Smith and Cornelius P. Cotter, *Power of the President During a Crisis* (Washington, D.C.: Public Affairs Press, 1960).

6. See Kallenback, p. 491.

7. See an account of his experience related in C. Hermann Pritchett, *The American Constitution* (New York: McGraw-Hill Book Co., 1968), p. 358.

8. Taken from the letters of John Hay and quoted in Pritchett, p. 358.

9. The vote was House: 416–0 and Senate: 88–2. For a critical account of the administration's version of the episode, see Joseph C. Gouldner, *Truth is the First Casualty* (Chicago: Rand McNally and Co., 1969).

10. See *Congressional Record*, 88th Congress, 2nd Session (August 7, 1964), 17967.

11. For such analysis, see George E. Reedy, *The Twilight of the Presidency* (New York: World Publishing Co., 1970), pp. 127–30 and Dorothy Buckton James, *The Contemporary Presidency* (New York: Pegasus Books, 1969), p. 144.

12. See the New York *Times* (June 26, 1969), p. 1.

13. See episode related in Kallenback, pp. 538–40.

14. For this function, see Roger Hilsman, *To Move a Nation* (Garden City, N.Y.: Doubleday and Co., 1967), pp. 558–59.

15. Ibid., p. 558.

16. Ibid., Chapter 35 for a discussion of this process.

17. Ibid., p. 542; for some dangers of this type of decision-making, see Reedy, pp. 10–15.

18. Ibid., p. 543.

19. For an insider's view, see Robert F. Kennedy, *Thirteen Days* (New York: W. W. Norton and Co., 1969).

20. See Gabriel A. Almond, *The American People and Foreign Policy* (New York: Frederick A. Praeger, 1961), p. 72.

21. See Sidney Verba, *et al.*, "Public Opinion and the War in Vietnam," *American Political Science Review*, June 1967, 331.

22. See James, p. 140.

23. See Verba, p. 333.

24. Ibid.

25. See the discussion in V. O. Key, *Public Opinion and American Democracy* (New York: Alfred A. Knopf, 1967), pp. 256–58.

26. See Aaron Wildavsky, "The Two Presidencies," *Transaction*, December 1966, 10.

27. For an interesting analysis of the role of ethnic groups in the making of American policy toward the Middle East, see the New York *Times*, April 6, 1970, 1.

28. See Wildavsky, p. 14.

29. For criticisms of the way the State Department performs its role, see James, pp. 148–50. One critic exasperated by the department was President John Kennedy who was alleged to have characterized it as a "bowl of jelly." Cited in Arthur M. Schlesinger, jr., *A Thousand Days* (Boston: Houghton Mifflin Co., 1965), p. 413.

30. For an interesting account of the role of presidential staff in a decision to deploy a limited antiballistic missile system, see the New York *Times*, March 19, 1969, 22.

7

CONCLUSION

☆☆☆☆☆

In the preceding chapters we have reviewed the functions of the president in the American political system. Such an examination indicates that the president performs a number of functions in the system. And these functions are closely interrelated rather than being discrete. The president also shares these functions with other institutions since the political process is too complex and untidy to fit into exact compartments.

It is also evident that the presidency is an evolving, rather than a static, institution. Its tasks and responsibilities have increased considerably since it was established. Indeed its functions are a mixture of traditional ones and those newly acquired and unheard of in previous decades. Such changes are a product of many forces. First, the presidency is subject to the influence of personality. To an extent any president gives to the office the imprint of his own character and personality. The presidency has also been shaped by its interaction with other participants in the policy process, such as Congress, the courts and the bureaucracy. Indeed, in this age of a vast welfare state one of the great challenges to any president may be the attempt to hold the bureaucracy accountable.

Like other institutions, the presidency has also been conditioned by the forces and pressures that affect society generally. As the country has been transformed into a major industrial world power, presidential tasks have become even more varied and complex. Public expectations about the president and what he can do or should do have similarly increased. Indeed, given the centrality and visibility of this position, the burdens imposed on it have been even greater than those imposed on other institutions.

On the whole, the presidency has been a fairly flexible and adaptable institution. It has adapted to meet many of the new demands. For example, originally selected by a few, the president is now popularly elected. While many nineteenth-century presidents regarded themselves primarily as administrators, recent presidents have performed a greater variety of functions ranging from chief legislator, guardian of domestic peace to manager of prosperity.

Nor have we seen the end of this evolutionary process. The presidency will likely remain the focus of increased demands and expectations, as the nation and the world are subject to changes, often of a turbulent character. Indeed, the presidency may have reached another critical point in its evolutionary process. Its tasks and duties are so varied and complex and their performance of such significance to the nation and the world that it has become one of the most powerful positions in the world. Yet at the same time, the circumstances of the age has subjected the president's leadership, domestic and international, to many limitations. Although a pivotal figure in world affairs, he is also constrained in ways unknown to his predecessors. While his powers may seem vast, measured against the problems to be confronted, they are not so vast. And as a repository of high public hopes and expectations, presidential actions or inactions inevitably disillusion some.

In the 1970s many basic institutions of the American system have come under criticism and reexamination. The presidency has not been excluded. Given its visibility and centrality, it is the main target of many. While some criticisms are ill-informed, misdirected or destructive in intent, others are serious efforts to deal with real problems. The answers provided by such a search and examination may well determine the future viability not only of the office but the political system as well.

BIBLIOGRAPHY

For more information or greater detail on any of the material treated in this book, the reader should consult the following works listed by topic; asterisks indicate availability in paperback. The references cited in the Notes for each chapter should also prove helpful.

GENERAL WORKS ON THE PRESIDENCY

* BAILEY, THOMAS A. *Presidential Greatness: The Image and the Man from George Washington to the Present.* New York: Appleton-Century-Crofts, 1966.

BINKLEY, WILFRED W. *The Man in the White House.* Baltimore: Johns Hopkins Press, 1959.

BROWN, STUART G. *The American Presidency.* New York: The Macmillan Co., 1966.

BROWNLOW, LOUIS. *The President and the Presidency.* Chicago: Public Administration Service, 1949.

* BURNS, JAMES MACGREGOR. *Presidential Government.* Boston: Houghton Mifflin Co., 1960.

* CORWIN, EDWARD S. *The President: Office and Powers.* New York: New York University Press, 1958.

COYLE, DAVID C. *The Ordeal of the Presidency.* Washington, D.C.: Public Affairs Press, 1960.

FINER, HERMAN. *The Presidency: Crisis and Regeneration.* Chicago: University of Chicago Press, 1960.

HYMAN, SIDNEY. *The American President.* New York: Harper and Row, Inc., 1954.

* JOHNSON, DONALD and JACK L. WALKER, eds., *The Dynamics of the American Presidency.* New York: John Wiley & Son, 1964.

* JOHNSON, WALTER. *1600 Pennsylvania Avenue.* Boston: Little, Brown, and Co., 1960.

KALLENBACK, JOSEPH. *The American Chief Executive.* New York: Harper and Row, Inc., 1966.

* KOENIG, LOUIS W. *The Chief Executive.* 2nd ed. New York: Harcourt, Brace and World, Inc., 1968.

* LASKI, HAROLD. *The American Presidency.* New York: Grosset and Dunlap, Inc., 1940.

* McCONNELL, GRANT. *The Modern Presidency.* New York: St. Martin's Press, 1967.

* ROSSITER, CLINTON. *The American Presidency.* New York: Harcourt, Brace, and World, Inc., 1960.

TOURTELLET, ARTHUR B. *The Presidents and the Presidency.* Garden City, N.Y.: Doubleday and Co., 1964.

TUGWELL, REXFORD G. *The Enlargement of the Presidency.* Garden City, N.Y.: Doubleday and Co., 1960.

* WARREN, SIDNEY, ed. *The American President.* Englewood Cliffs, N.J.: Prentice-Hall, 1967.

WILDAVSKY, AARON, *The Presidency.* Boston: Little, Brown and Co., 1969.

PRESIDENTIAL POWER AND DECISION-MAKING

BLACKMAN, JOHN L., JR. *Presidential Seizures in Labor Disputes.* Cambridge: Harvard University Press, 1967.

CORNWELL, ELMER E., JR. *Presidential Leadership of Public Opinion.* Bloomington: Indiana University Press, 1965.

* HARGROVE, ERWIN C. *Presidential Leadership: Personality and Political Style.* New York: The Macmillan Co., 1966.

HERRING, PENDLETON. *Presidential Leadership.* New York: W. W. Norton and Co., 1965.

KOENIG, LOUIS W. *The Presidency and Crisis: Powers of the Office from the Invasion of Poland to Pearl Harbor.* New York: King's Crown Press, 1944.

LONGAKER, RICHARD P. *The Presidency and Individual Liberties.* Ithaca: Cornell University Press, 1961.

MAY, ERNEST R. *The Ultimate Decision: The President as Commander in Chief.* New York: George Braziller, Inc., 1960.

MORRIS, RICHARD B. *Great Presidential Decisions.* Philadelphia: J. B. Lippincott Co., 1965.

* NEUSTADT, RICHARD E. *Presidential Power.* New York: New American Library, 1964.

SCHUBERT, GLENDON A. *The Presidency in the Courts.* Minneapolis: University of Minnesota Press, 1957.

SMITH, JOHN MALCOLM, and CORNELIUS P. COTTER. *Powers of the President During Crises.* Washington, D.C.: Public Affairs Press, 1960.

* SORENSEN, THEODORE C. *Decision-Making in the White House.* New York: Columbia University Press, 1964.

* WARREN, SIDNEY. *The President as World Leader.* Philadelphia: J. B. Lippincott Co., 1964.

PRESIDENTIAL STAFF

* FENNO, RICHARD F. *The President's Cabinet.* New York: Random House, 1959.

FLASH, EDWARD S., JR. *Economic Advice and Presidential Leadership: The Council of Economic Advisors.* New York: Columbia University Press, 1965.

HOBBS, EDWARD HENRY, *Behind the President: A Study of Executive Office Agencies.* Washington, D.C.: Public Affairs Press, 1954.

KOENIG, LOUIS, *The Invisible Presidency.* New York: Holt, Rinehart and Winston, Inc. 1960.

NEUSTADT, RICHARD E. "Approaches to Staffing the Presidency," *American Political Science Review,* December 1963, 855–64; June 1964, 398–400.

SILVERMAN, CORINNE, *The President's Economic Advisors: Inter-University Case #48.* University, Ala.: University of Alabama Press, 1959.

ELECTORAL ARENA FOR THE PRESIDENCY

BEHN, ROBERT D., ed. *The Lessons of Victory* (Ripon Society). New York: Dial Press, 1969.

* CHESTER, LEWIS, GODFREY HODGSON, and BRUCE PAGE. *An American Melodrama.* New York: Viking Press, 1969.

* DAVIS, JAMES, *Presidential·Primaries: Road to the White House.* New York: Thomas Y. Crowell Co., 1967.

MOOS, MALCOLM, *Politics, Presidents and Coattails.* Baltimore: Johns Hopkins University Press, 1950.

* PEIRCE, NEAL R. *The People's President.* New York: Simon and Schuster, 1968.

* POLSBY, NELSON and AARON WILDAVSKY. *Presidential Elections.* 2nd ed. New York: Charles Scribner's Sons, 1968.

* POMPER, GERALD, *Nominating the President,* Evanston: Northwestern University Press, 1963.

ROSEBOOM, EUGENE, *A History of Presidential Elections.* Rev. ed. New York: The Macmillan Co., 1964.

* WHITE, THEODORE, *The Making of the President 1960.* New York: Atheneum, 1961.

* ———, *The Making of the President 1964.* New York: Atheneum, 1965.

* ———, *The Making of the President 1968.* New York: Atheneum, 1969. For a critical and challenging review of White's book, see Bill D. Moyers, "The Election in the Year of Decay," *Saturday Review,* August 9, 1969, 23.

THE PRESIDENT AND THE CONGRESS

* BINKLEY, WILFRED E., *The President and Congress.* New York: Random House, 1962.

CHAMBERLAIN, LAWRENCE H. *The President, Congress and Legislation.* New York: Columbia University Press, 1946.

NEUSTADT, RICHARD W. "The Presidency and Legislation: The Growth of Central Clearance," *American Political Science Review,* September 1954, 641–71.

NEUSTADT, RICHARD E. "The Presidency and Legislation: Planning the President's Program," *American Political Science Review,* December 1955, 980–1020.

TRUMAN, DAVID B. "The Presidency and Congressional Leadership: Some Notes on our Changing Constitution," *American Philosophy Society Proceedings,* October 15, 1959, 687–92.

PRESIDENT AND THE BUREAUCRACY

* BLAU, PETER. *Bureaucracy in Modern Society.* New York: Random House, 1956.

* FREEMAN, J. LEIPER. *The Political Process.* New York: Random House, 1955.

HOLDEN, MATTHEW, JR. "Imperialism in Bureaucracy," *American Political Science Review,* December 1966, 659–74.

* JACOB, CHARLES E. *Policy and Bureaucracy.* Princeton: D. Van Nostrand Co., 1966.

* ROURKE, FRANCIS. *Bureaucratic Power in National Politics.* Boston: Little, Brown and Co., 1965.

SAYRE, WALLACE, ed. *The Federal Service.* Englewood Cliffs, N.J.: Prentice-Hall, 1965.

TULLOCK, GORDON. *The Politics of Bureaucracy.* Washington, D.C.: Public Affairs Press, 1965.

WANN, A. J. *The President as Chief Administrator: A Study of F. D. R.* Washington, D.C.: Public Affairs Press, 1968.

PRESIDENTS SINCE 1933

FRANKLIN D. ROOSEVELT

* BURNS, JAMES MACGREGOR. *Roosevelt: The Lion and the Fox.* New York: Harcourt, Brace and World, Inc., 1959.

FARLEY, JAMES. *Jim Farley's Story.* New York: Whittlesey House, 1945.

* LEUCHTENBURG, WILLIAM E. *Franklin D. Roosevelt and the New Deal.* New York: Harper and Row, Inc., 1963.

* PERKINS, FRANCES. *The Roosevelt I Knew.* New York: Viking Press, 1946.

RAUCH, BASIL. *Roosevelt: From Munich to Pearl Harbor.* New York: Creative Age Press, 1950.

ROLLINS, ALFRED B. *Roosevelt and Howe.* New York: Alfred A. Knopf, 1962.

ROSEMAN, SAMUEL I. *Working with Roosevelt.* New York: Harper and Row, Inc., 1952.

* SCHLESINGER, ARTHUR M., JR. *The Age of Roosevelt.* Boston: Houghton Mifflin Co., 1957.

SHERWOOD, ROBERT. *Roosevelt and Hopkins.* New York: Grosset and Dunlap, Inc., 1950.

* TUGWELL, REXFORD G. *The Democratic Roosevelt.* Garden City, N.Y.: Doubleday and Co., 1957.

HARRY S. TRUMAN

* BERNSTEIN, BARTON J. and MATUSOW, ALLEN J., eds. *The Truman Administration: A Documentary History.* New York: Harper and Row, Inc., 1966.

DAVIES, RICHARD D. *Housing Reform During the Truman Administration.* Columbia, Mo.: University of Missouri Press, 1966.

KIRKENDALL, R. S., ed. *The Truman Period as a Research Field.* Columbia: University of Missouri Press, 1968.

* PHILLIPS, CABELL. *The Truman Presidency.* New York: The Macmillan Co., 1966.

* ROSS, IRWIN. *The Loneliest Campaign: The Truman Victory of 1948.* New York: New American Library, 1968.

SPANIER, JOHN W. *The Truman-MacArthur Controversy and the Korean War.* New York: W. W. Norton and Co., 1965.

STEINBERG, ALFRED. *The Man from Missouri: The Life and Times of Harry S. Truman.* New York: G. P. Putnam's Sons, 1962.

* TRUMAN, HARRY S. *Memoirs.* 2 vols. New York: New American Library, 1968.

DWIGHT D. EISENHOWER

ADAMS, SHERMAN. *Firsthand Report.* New York: Harper and Row, Inc., 1961.

ANDERSON, JOHN W. *Eisenhower, Brownell and the Congress.* University, Ala.: University of Alabama Press, 1964.

* DONOVAN, ROBERT J. *Eisenhower: The Inside Story.* New York: Harper and Row, Inc., 1956.

EISENHOWER, DWIGHT D. *The White House Years: Mandate for Change 1953–1956.* New York: New American Library, 1965.

HUGHES, EMMET J. *The Ordeal of Power.* New York: Atheneum, 1963.

ROVERE, RICHARD. *The Eisenhower Years.* New York: Farrar, Straus and Cudahy, 1956.

JOHN F. KENNEDY

HARRIS, SEYMOUR E. *The Economics of the Kennedy Years.* New York: Harper and Row, Inc., 1964.

* HILSMAN, ROGER. *To Move a Nation.* Garden City, N.Y.: Doubleday and Co., 1967.

* SCHLESINGER, ARTHUR M., JR. *A Thousand Days: John F. Kennedy in the White House.* New York: Houghton Mifflin Co., 1965.

* SORENSEN, THEODORE C. *Kennedy.* New York: Harper and Row, Inc., 1965.

LYNDON B. JOHNSON

AMRINE, MICHAEL. *The Awesome Challenge: The Hundred Days of Lyndon Johnson.* New York: G. P. Putnam's Sons, 1964.

BURNS, JAMES MACGREGOR, ed. *To Heal and to Build: The Programs of President Lyndon B. Johnson.* New York: McGraw-Hill Book Co., Inc., 1968.

* EVANS, ROLAND, and ROBERT NOVAK. *Lyndon B. Johnson: Exercise of Power.* New York: New American Library, 1968.

GEYELIN, PHILIP. *Lyndon B. Johnson and the World.* New York: Frederick A. Praeger, 1966.

ROBERTS, CHARLES W. *LBJ's Inner Circle.* New York: Dial Press, 1965.

* WICKER, TOM. *JFK and LBJ: The Influence of Personality on Politics.* New York: William Morrow and Co., Inc., 1968.

RICHARD M. NIXON

COSTELLO, WILLIAM. *The Facts About Nixon: An Unauthorized Biography.* New York: Viking Press, 1960.

KRAUS, SIDNEY, ed. *The Great Debates: Background, Perspective, Effects.* Bloomington: Indiana University Press, 1962.

* MAZO, EARL, and STEPHEN HESS. *Nixon: A Political Portrait.* New York: Harper and Row, Inc., 1969.

* NIXON, RICHARD M. *Six Crises.* Garden City, N.Y.: Doubleday and Co., 1962.

There are also a number of public documents and privately published reference materials on the presidency that the reader will find valuable. Many are available in a college or university library:

The Public Papers of the President is an annual volume published by the National Archives and Records Service since the Truman Administration and will continue for future presidents. The public papers of Franklin D. Roosevelt have been privately published for the years of his presidency (1933–1945). Prior to that time, one can consult James D. Richardson, *Messages and Papers of the President*, 1789–1897 (ten volumes) for a partial collection. Presidential papers for the period 1897–1945 were published in a number of cases by private publishers. See Laurence F. Schmeckebier and Roy B. Eastin, *Government Publications and Their Use* (Washington, D.C.: The Brookings Institution, 1969), p. 334.

For the texts of presidential State of the Union Messages, see *The State of the Union Messages 1790–1966,* ed. Fred Israel (New York: Chelsea House, 1967). House Document 218 (87th Congress) contains the Inaugural Addresses from George Washington to John F. Kennedy. The General Services Administration publishes *A Weekly Compilation of Presidential Documents,* published every Monday since August 1965. Included are transcripts of news conferences, messages to Congress, public speeches, remarks and statements.

A good source on the structure, powers and functions of the executive branch is the *United States Government Organizational Manual,* published annually by the Government Printing Office.

For provisions of laws enacted during an administration, see the *United States Statutes at Large,* wherein bills are listed in chronological order by Congress and Session. Laws are listed by subject matter in the *United States Code.* Annual supplements are issued and there is an overall revision every six years. Since 1950, treaties can be found in *United States Treaties and Other International Agreements,* a publication of the Department of State. Prior to that time, they were included in the *United States Statutes at Large.*

The regulations of executive agencies and executive orders are published in the *Federal Register,* published five times weekly by the National Archives and Records Service.

Executive agencies, as well as the president, issue a variety of documents on diverse topics. These items are listed in the *Monthly Catalog of Government Publications.* For other sources and direction in how to use them, see Laurence F. Schmeckebier, *et al., Government Publications and Their Use,* previously cited.

For election data, one can consult *America at the Polls* (1920–

1964), compiled and edited by Richard Scammon (Pittsburgh: Governmental Affairs Institute, University of Pittsburgh, 1965).

Another excellent source of information are the publications of Congressional Quarterly, a private reporting service. Its *Weekly Report* contains a good deal of material related to the presidency, such as messages, legislative proposals, appointments, etc. Its annual *Almanac* is also valuable. One might also consult its mammoth *Congress and the Nation*, Vol. I (1945–1964) and Vol. II (1965–1968) which spans six presidencies and is an encyclopedia of data. A number of its special reports are also relevant, such as *The Presidential Nominating Conventions* (1968), *Nixon, The First Year of His Presidency* and *Historical Review of Presidential Candidates* (5th ed.).

Finally a good daily newspaper, such as the New York *Times* or the Washington *Post,* is a valuable source of current developments.

APPENDIX A

CONSTITUTIONAL PROVISIONS
RELATED TO THE PRESIDENCY

ARTICLE II

Section 1. (1). The executive power shall be vested in a President of the United States of America. He shall hold his office during the term of four years,[1] and, together with the Vice President, chosen for the same term, be elected, as follows:

(2). Each State shall appoint, in such manner as the legislature thereof may direct, a number of electors, equal to the whole number of Senators and Representatives to which the State may be entitled in the Congress: but no Senator or Representative, or person holding an office of trust or profit under the United States, shall be appointed an elector.

The electors shall meet in their respective States,[2] and vote by ballot for two persons, of whom one at least shall not be an inhabitant of the same State with themselves. And they shall make a list of all the persons voted for, and of the number of votes for each; which list they shall sign and certify, and transmit sealed to

[1] Qualified, as to length of service, by the 22nd Amendment.
[2] The 12th Amendment (1804) superseded the provisions of this paragraph, and the 12th Amendment is modified by the 20th.

193

the seat of the government of the United States, directed to the president of the Senate. The president of the Senate shall, in the presence of the Senate and House of Representatives, open all the certificates, and the votes shall then be counted. The person having the greatest number of votes shall be the President, if such number be a majority of the whole number of electors appointed; and if there be more than one who have such majority, and have an equal number of votes, then the House of Representatives shall immediately choose by ballot one of them for President; and if no person have a majority, then from the five highest on the list the said House shall in like manner choose the President. But in choosing the President, the votes shall be taken by States, the representation from each State having one vote; a quorum for this purpose shall consist of a member or members from two thirds of the States, and a majority of all the States shall be necessary to a choice. In every case, after the choice of the President, the person having the greatest number of votes of the electors shall be the Vice President. But if there should remain two or more who have equal votes, the Senate shall choose from them by ballot the Vice President.

(3). The Congress may determine the time of choosing the electors, and the day on which they shall give their votes; which day shall be the same throughout the United States.

(4). No person except a natural born citizen, or a citizen of the United States, at the time of the adoption of this Constitution, shall be eligible to the office of President; neither shall any person be eligible to that office who shall not have attained to the age of thirty five years, and been fourteen years a resident within the United States.

(5). In case of the removal of the President from office,[3] or of his death, resignation, or inability to discharge the powers and duties of the said office, the same shall devolve on the Vice President, and the Congress may by law provide for the case of removal, death, resignation or inability, both of the President and Vice President, declaring what officer shall then act as President, and such officer shall act accordingly, until the disability be removed, or a President shall be elected.

[3] The provisions of this paragraph are clarified by the 25th Amendment.

(6). The President shall, at stated times, receive for his services, a compensation, which shall neither be increased nor diminished during the period for which he shall have been elected, and he shall not receive within that period any other emolument from the United States, or any of them.

(7). Before he enter on the execution of his office, he shall take the following oath or affirmation:—"I do solemnly swear (or affirm) that I will faithfully execute the office of President of the United States, and will to the best of my ability, preserve, protect and defend the Constitution of the United States."

Section 2. (1). The President shall be commander in chief of the army and navy of the United States, and of the militia of the several States, when called into the actual service of the United States; he may require the opinion, in writing, of the principal officer in each of the executive departments, upon any subject relating to the duties of their respective offices, and he shall have power to grant reprieves and pardons for offenses against the United States, except in cases of impeachment.

(2). He shall have power, by and with the advice and consent of the Senate, to make treaties, provided two thirds of the Senators present concur; and he shall nominate, and by and with the advice and consent of the Senate, shall appoint ambassadors, other public ministers and consuls, judges of the Supreme Court, and all other officers of the United States, whose appointments are not herein otherwise provided for, and which shall be established by law: but the Congress may by law vest the appointment of such inferior officers, as they think proper, in the President alone, in the courts of law, or in the heads of departments.

(3). The President shall have power to fill up all vacancies that may happen during the recess of the Senate, by granting commissions which shall expire at the end of their next session.

Section 3. He shall from time to time give to the Congress information of the state of the Union, and recommend to their consideration such measures as he shall judge necessary and expedient; he may, on extraordinary occasions, convene both Houses, or either of them, and in case of disagreement between them, with respect to the time of adjournment, he may adjourn them to such time as he shall think proper; he shall receive ambassadors and other public ministers; he shall take care that the laws be faithfully executed, and shall commission all the officers of the United States.

Section 4. The President, Vice President and all civil officers of the United States, shall be removed from office on impeachment for, and conviction of, treason, bribery, or other high crimes and misdemeanors.

☆

OTHER RELEVANT PARTS

ARTICLE I

Section 3. (Senate) (4). The Vice-President of the United States shall be President of the Senate, but shall have no vote, unless they be equally divided.

(5). The Senate shall choose their other officers, and also a President *pro tempore,* in the absence of the Vice-President, or when he shall exercise the office of President of the United States.

(6). The Senate shall have the sole power to try all impeachments. When sitting for that purpose, they shall be on oath or affirmation.

Section 6. (2). No Senator or Representative shall, during the time for which he was elected, be appointed to any civil office under the authority of the United States, which shall have been created, or the emoluments whereof shall have been increased, during such time; and no person holding any office under the United States shall be a member of either house during his continuance in office.

Section 7. (Method of Making Laws) (1). All bills for raising revenue shall originate in the House of Representatives; but the

Senate may propose or concur with amendments as on other bills.

(2). Every bill which shall have passed the House of Representatives and the Senate, shall, before it become a law, be presented to the President of the United States; if he approve he shall sign it, but if not he shall return it with his objections to that house in which it shall have originated, who shall enter the objections at large on their journal, and proceed to reconsider it. If after such reconsideration two-thirds of that house shall agree to pass the bill, it shall be sent, together with the objections, to the other house, by which it shall likewise be reconsidered, and, if approved by two thirds of that house, it shall become a law. But in all such cases the votes of both houses shall be determined by yeas and nays, and the names of the persons voting for and against the bill shall be centered on the journal of each house respectively. If any bill shall not be returned by the President within ten days (Sundays excepted) after it shall have been presented to him, the same shall be a law, in like manner as if he had signed it, unless the Congress by their adjournment prevent its return, in which case it shall not be a law.

(3). Every order, resolution, or vote to which the concurrence of the Senate and House of Representatives may be necessary (except on a question of adjournment) shall be presented to the President of the United States; and before the same shall take effect, shall be approved by him, or being disapproved by him, shall be repassed by two thirds of the Senate and House of Representatives, according to the rules and limitations prescribed in the case of a bill.

☆

AMENDMENTS

ARTICLE XII [4]

The electors shall meet in their respective States and vote by ballot for President and Vice President, one of whom, at least, shall not be an inhabitant of the same State with themselves; they shall name in their ballots the person voted for as President, and in dis-

[4] Adopted in 1804.

tinct ballots the person voted for as Vice President, and they shall make distinct lists of all persons voted for as President, and of all persons voted for as Vice President, and of the number of votes for each, which lists they shall sign and certify, and transmit sealed to the seat of the government of the United States, directed to the president of the Senate;—The president of the Senate shall, in the presence of the Senate and House of Representatives, open all the certificates and the votes shall then be counted;—The person having the greatest number of votes for President, shall be the President, if such number be a majority of the whole number of electors appointed; and if no person have such majority, then from the persons having the highest numbers not exceeding three on the list of those voted for as President, the House of Representatives shall choose immediately, by ballot, the President. But in choosing the President, the votes shall be taken by States, the representation from each State having one vote; a quorum for this purpose shall consist of a member or members from two-thirds of the States, and a majority of all the States shall be necessary to a choice. And if the House of Representatives shall not choose a President whenever the right of choice shall devolve upon them, before the fourth day of March next following,[5] then the Vice President shall act as President, as in the case of the death or other constitutional disability of the President.—The person having the greatest number of votes as Vice President, shall be the Vice President, if such number be a majority of the whole number of electors appointed, and if no person have a majority, then from the two highest numbers on the list, the Senate shall choose the Vice President; a quorum for the purpose shall consist of two-thirds of the whole number of Senators, and a majority of the whole number shall be necessary to a choice. But no person constitutionally ineligible to the office of President shall be eligible to that of Vice President of the United States.

ARTICLE XX[6]

Section 1. The terms of the President and Vice President shall end

---

[5] Modified by the 20th Amendment.
[6] Adopted in 1933.

at noon on the 20th day of January, and the terms of Senators and Representatives at noon on the 3d day of January, of the years in which such terms would have ended if this article had not been ratified; and the terms of their successors shall then begin.

Section 2. The Congress shall assemble at least once in every year, and such meeting shall begin at noon on the 3d day of January, unless they shall by law appoint a different day.

Section 3. If, at the time fixed for the beginning of the term of the President, the President-elect shall have died, the Vice President-elect shall become President. If a President shall not have been chosen before the time fixed for the beginning of his term, or if the President-elect shall have failed to qualify, then the Vice President-elect shall act as President until a President shall have qualified; and the Congress may by law provide for the case wherein neither a President-elect nor a Vice President-elect shall have qualified, declaring who shall then act as President, or the manner in which one who is to act shall be selected, and such person shall act accordingly until a President or Vice President shall have qualified.

Section 4. The Congress may by law provide for the case of the death of any of the persons from whom the House of Representatives may choose a President whenever the right of choice shall have devolved upon them, and for the case of the death of any of the persons from whom the Senate may choose a Vice President whenever the right of choice shall have devolved upon them.

Section 5. Sections 1 and 2 shall take effect on the 15th day of October following the ratification of this article.

Section 6. This article shall be inoperative unless it shall have been ratified as an amendment to the Constitution by the legislatures of three-fourths of the several States within seven years from the date of its submission.

ARTICLE XXII [7]

Section 1. No person shall be elected to the office of the President more than twice, and no person who has held the office of President, or acted as President, for more than two years of a term to which some other person was elected President shall be elected to the office of the President more than once. But this Article shall not apply to any person holding the office of President when this Article was proposed by the Congress, and shall not prevent any person who may be holding the office of President, or acting as President, during the term within which this Article becomes operative from holding the office of President or acting as President during the remainder of such term.

Section 2. This Article shall be inoperative unless it shall have been ratified as an amendment to the Constitution by the legislatures of three-fourths of the several States within seven years from the date of its submission to the States by the Congress.

ARTICLE XXIII [8]

Section 1. The District constituting the seat of Government of the United States shall appoint in such manner as the Congress may direct:

A number of electors of President and Vice President equal to the whole number of Senators and Representatives in Congress to which the District would be entitled if it were a State, but in no event more than the least populous State; they shall be in addition to those appointed by the States, but they shall be considered, for the purposes of the election of President and Vice President, to be electors appointed by a State; and they shall meet in the District and perform such duties as provided by the twelfth article of amendment.

Section 2. The Congress shall have power to enforce this article by appropriate legislation.

[7] Adopted in 1951.
[8] Adopted in 1961.

ARTICLE XXIV [9]

Section 1. The right of citizens of the United States to vote in any primary or other election for President or Vice President, for electors for President or Vice President, or for Senator or Representative in Congress, shall not be denied or abridged by the United States or any State by reason of failure to pay any poll tax or other tax.

Section 2. The Congress shall have power to enforce this article by appropriate legislation.

ARTICLE XXV [10]

Section 1. In case of the removal of the President from office or of his death or resignation, the Vice President shall become President.

Section 2. Whenever there is a vacancy in the office of the Vice President, the President shall nominate a Vice President who shall take office upon confirmation by a majority vote of both Houses of Congress.

Section 3. Whenever the President transmits to the president pro tempore of the Senate and the Speaker of the House of Representatives his written declaration that he is unable to discharge the powers and duties of his office, and until he transmits to them a written declaration to the contrary, such powers and duties shall be discharged by the Vice President as Acting President.

Section 4. Whenever the Vice President and a majority of either the principal officers of the executive departments or of such other body as Congress may by law provide, transmit to the president pro tempore of the Senate and the Speaker of the House of Representatives their written declaration that the President is unable to discharge the powers and duties of his office, the Vice President

[9] Adopted in 1964.
[10] Adopted in 1967.

shall immediately assume the powers and duties of the office as Acting President.

Thereafter, when the President transmits to the president pro tempore of the Senate and the Speaker of the House of Representatives his written declaration that no inability exists, he shall resume the powers and duties of his office unless the Vice President and a majority of either the principal officers of the executive department or of such other body as Congress may by law provide, transmit within four days to the president pro tempore of the Senate and the Speaker of the House of Representatives their written declaration that the President is unable to discharge the powers and duties of his office. Thereupon Congress shall decide the issue, assembling within forty-eight hours for that purpose if not in session. If the Congress, within twenty-one days after receipt of the latter written declaration, or, if Congress is not in session, within twenty-one days after Congress is required to assemble, determines by two-thirds vote of both Houses that the President is unable to discharge the powers and duties of his office, the Vice President shall continue to discharge the same as Acting President; otherwise, the President shall resume the powers and duties of his office.

APPENDIX B

☆☆☆☆☆

PRESIDENTS OF THE UNITED STATES

		Party	Term
1.	George Washington	Federalist	1789–1797
2.	John Adams	Federalist	1797–1801
3.	Thomas Jefferson	Democratic-Republican	1801–1809
4.	James Madison	Democratic-Republican	1809–1817
5.	James Monroe	Democratic-Republican	1817–1825
6.	John Quincy Adams	Democratic-Republican	1825–1829
7.	Andrew Jackson	Democratic	1829–1837
8.	Martin Van Buren	Democratic	1837–1841
9.	William Henry Harrison	Whig	1841
10.	John Tyler	Whig	1841–1845
11.	James K. Polk	Democratic	1845–1849
12.	Zachary Taylor	Whig	1849–1850
13.	Millard Fillmore	Whig	1850–1853
14.	Franklin Pierce	Democratic	1853–1857
15.	James Buchanan	Democratic	1857–1861
16.	Abraham Lincoln	Republican	1861–1865
17.	Andrew Johnson	National Union	1865–1869
18.	Ulysses S. Grant	Republican	1869–1877
19.	Rutherford B. Hayes	Republican	1877–1881
20.	James A. Garfield	Republican	1881
21.	Chester A. Arthur	Republican	1881–1885
22.	Grover Cleveland	Democratic	1885–1889

23.	Benjamin Harrison	Republican	1889–1893
24.	Grover Cleveland	Democratic	1893–1897
25.	William McKinley	Republican	1897–1901
26.	Theodore Roosevelt	Republican	1901–1909
27.	William Howard Taft	Republican	1909–1913
28.	Woodrow Wilson	Democratic	1913–1921
29.	Warren G. Harding	Republican	1921–1923
30.	Calvin Coolidge	Republican	1923–1929
31.	Herbert Hoover	Republican	1929–1933
32.	Franklin Delano Roosevelt	Democratic	1933–1945
33.	Harry S. Truman	Democratic	1945–1953
34.	Dwight D. Eisenhower	Republican	1953–1961
35.	John F. Kennedy	Democratic	1961–1963
36.	Lyndon B. Johnson	Democratic	1963–1969
37.	Richard M. Nixon	Republican	1969–

VICE-PRESIDENTS OF THE UNITED STATES

		Party	Term
1.	John Adams	Federalist	1789–1797
2.	Thomas Jefferson	Democratic-Republican	1797–1801
3.	Aaron Burr	Democratic-Republican	1801–1805
4.	George Clinton	Democratic-Republican	1805-1812
5.	Elbridge Gerry	Democratic-Republican	1813–1814
6.	Daniel D. Tompkins	Democratic-Republican	1817–1825
7.	John C. Calhoun	Democratic-Republican	1825–1832
8.	Martin Van Buren	Democratic	1833–1837
9.	Richard M. Johnson	Democratic	1837–1841
10.	John Tyler	Whig	1841
11.	George M. Dallas	Democratic	1845–1849
12.	Millard Fillmore	Whig	1849–1850
13.	William R. King	Democratic	1853
14.	John C. Breckinridge	Democratic	1857–1861
15.	Hannibal Hamlin	Republican	1861–1865
16.	Andrew Johnson	National Union	1865
17.	Schuyler Colfax	Republican	1869–1873
18.	Henry Wilson	Republican	1873–1875
19.	William A. Wheeler	Republican	1877–1881
20.	Chester A. Arthur	Republican	1881
21.	Thomas A. Hendricks	Democratic	1885
22.	Levi P. Morton	Republican	1889–1893

23.	Adlai E. Stevenson	Democratic	1893–1897
24.	Garret A. Hobart	Republican	1897–1899
25.	Theodore Roosevelt	Republican	1901
26.	Charles W. Fairbanks	Republican	1905–1909
27.	James S. Sherman	Republican	1909–1912
28.	Thomas R. Marshall	Democratic	1913–1921
29.	Calvin Coolidge	Republican	1921–1923
30.	Charles G. Dawes	Republican	1925–1929
31.	Charles Curtis	Republican	1929–1933
32.	John N. Garner	Democratic	1933–1941
33.	Henry A. Wallace	Democratic	1941–1945
34.	Harry S. Truman	Democratic	1945
35.	Alben W. Barkley	Democratic	1949–1953
36.	Richard M. Nixon	Republican	1953–1961
37.	Lyndon B. Johnson	Democratic	1961–1963
38.	Hubert H. Humphrey	Democratic	1965–1969
39.	Spiro Agnew	Republican	1969–

INDEX

☆☆☆☆☆